What Others Are Saying

The Saboteur unmasks the diabolical schemes the kingdom of darkness has been using against mankind since the beginning of time. In Hosea 4:6, God declares, "My people are destroyed for lack of knowledge." Knowing God and understanding your adversary are both key in recognizing and dismantling strongholds. Heather Otis Tayloe does an excellent job in revealing these principles to her readers. This book is a must read for all believers!

Dr. G. Craig Lauterbach
Founder & President, Lifeword Publishing
Founder & President, CLM International

In Matthew 10:16, Jesus commands us to be "shrewd as snakes and innocent as doves." This is a call for His people to possess practical wisdom in understanding and anticipating how the enemy operates so that we can effectively take our stand against him, all while maintaining our integrity and purity of heart. In this exceptional book, *The Saboteur,* Heather Tayloe exposes the motives and methods of the devil and his army in a way that empowers us to fearlessly exercise the authority we have in Christ Jesus so that His victory can be experienced as our own!

Mary Soler
Biblical Teacher and Author, *Splendid Day*

You hold in your hand a prophetic exhortation prepared for you by Heather Tayloe. Heather is a clear prophetic voice in our generation. From her beginning days she was trained in the ways of the Lord. She is both sensitive to the voice of the Holy Spirit and true to the Holy Scriptures. She writes with a divine urgency to prepare God's people to navigate this present darkness. "Arise, shine; for your light has come! And the glory of the Lord is risen upon you. For behold, the darkness shall cover the earth, and deep darkness the people; but the Lord will arise over you, and His glory will be seen upon you" (Isaiah 60:1-2). If you have been looking for spiritual clarity exposing the unseen powers working among us, *The Saboteur* is a valuable manual for the last days.

Pastor Sharon Millier
Living Word Christian Center, Pendleton, Oregon

It seems sometimes we spend more time talking about issues than understanding what they are and how to solve them. In *The Saboteur*, Heather identifies deep needs concerning people's lives today and teaches biblical solutions. The world is desperate for the truths in God's Word, but doesn't know how to find the meaning behind the words. We want to know God but don't see our own barriers that keep us from Him. We have a real enemy intent on destroying every part of our lives. Heather addresses the challenges and offers real solutions to solve them. I do not recommend this book unless you are serious about true fulfillment in your life!

Dr. Kevin Dieckilman
CEO / President, One Heart for Israel

The Saboteur is more than a book. It is a plea by its author to understand that the evil one is real! This truth is being shunned, shrugged off, or casually overlooked by non-believers and believers alike. Heather Otis Tayloe recognizes that those in the Church are often not being equipped from the pulpit because the comfort zone of congregants is at risk. With a heart like Jesus and armed with Scripture, Ms. Tayloe urges the reader to wake up to the reality of satan as the saboteur who seeks to kill, steal, and destroy. He does not come parading a pitch fork with horns on his head. Rather he works in the dark corners of everyday life with the subtle tools of doubt, fear, mistrust, lust, greed, and power grabs. He enters our lives through unassuming gateways frequently found in social media, games, movies, and music, to name a few. We are often unaware that we are puppets, and he is pulling our strings. Ms. Tayloe admonishes that the only way to cut these ties and be free from the saboteur's grasp is to cling to Jesus and delve deep into the Word. *The Saboteur* is a wake-up call to those fully asleep and to those dozing behind the wheels of their lives. Once you've read it, you can't help but rise and shine in to a new awareness of the truth.

Michelle P. Griffith
Writer/Producer/Editor, Iron Image

There is a well-devised, well-coordinated, and pervasive lie among the people of God that the devil cannot touch us because we are confessing and committed Christians, thus untouchable by evil and its grotesque intentions! The result of this willful ignorance is, "My people are destroyed for lack of knowledge. Because you have rejected knowledge, I also will reject you from being priest for Me" (Hosea 4:6). *The Saboteur* by Heather Tayloe is a study exposing the works of the devil that have notoriously been ignored by the church for centuries. As a pastor and traveling evangelist for many years, I have seen the fear and skepticism among church leaders concerning the works of the devil and his relentless pursuits against Christ followers. Choosing ignorance of his tactics and a disdain to hear about this dark and tangled web, they choose to delete the passages of Scripture that evidences the truths concerning our fight against satan and his minions. I applaud Heather for taking this weight head on and writing *The Saboteur*. These truths have been concealed and ignored for far too long! All people of all ages should read this engaging and instructional book and learn how to fight with our prescribed weapons of warfare.

Pastor Lorraine Coconato
Leaves of Healing Ministries

THE SABOTEUR

Agent of Subterfuge and Subversive Stratagems

Heather Otis Tayloe

Dedication

I dedicate this book to my God—the Author and Finisher of all His work. I give all the glory to Your beloved name! There is no higher name under heaven or earth—none more powerful or more deserving of praise and worship than Jesus! I also dedicate this work to my beloved family—my husband and my three children. Even though I have written for decades, my family has never wavered in their support of me tackling this particular book. They have each helped me to see it through. Since this work has been personally costly, I needed the prayerful support of both my family and friends to finish it. This book is also a homage of sorts to my father's 1970s book, *Like a Roaring Lion,* which is now out of print. Knowing how important it was that I benefitted from their spiritual instruction, both of my parents instilled in me a rich heritage of understanding and prayer from my earliest days. Thank you!

> Looking unto Jesus, the author and finisher of our faith, who for the joy that was set before Him endured the cross, despising the shame, and has sat down at the right hand of the throne of God. (Hebrews 12:2)

Acknowledgments

Mary Soler, a dear friend, inspired me to complete this work through her pioneering publication about the bride of Christ, *Splendid Day*. Her courage and tenacity fueled my vision to finish what I knew needed to see the light of day.

My family has provided an unremitting covering of prayer, along with a proven personal support team marked by unwavering encouragement. United in spirit with my husband, John, our three children—Shane, Brittany, and Chase—and their spouses, this dream was brought to fruition.

I also want to specifically acknowledge my sister, April, whose beautiful support strengthened my heart to take on this book project. She has been a lifelong tender of my dreams and a marvelous cheerleader who encouraged me all the way to publication.

Finally, heartfelt recognition is due to my intrepid prayer partners and devoted students of God's blessed Word—Kathy, Judy, Karen, Angela, and Debbie—whose unrelenting encouragement strengthened my resolve to complete this work.

Contents

[Jesus] has gone into heaven and is at the right hand of God, angels and authorities and powers having been made subject to Him. (1 Peter 3:22)

Foreword

Have you noticed something strange in today's troubling headlines?

I realize a question like this is bound to elicit thoughts about conspiracies—deep State actors, hidden agendas, dark money. That sort of thing.

While human conspiracies may well exist, this answer fails to explain how activists, scholars, politicians, and preachers can correctly identify the consequences of today's problems and yet remain powerless to solve them. Hindrances and setbacks seem to be on a cruel loop, reappearing on our doorsteps with frustrating regularity.

In spite of our vaunted education and technology, crises have become quandaries. We celebrate progressive hopes and claims, but forward motion is almost nowhere to be seen. Strange indeed.

If societal voices are louder and more vitriolic, it is because after decades of attempting to solve ever growing problems we are failing. Miserably. Worse yet, no one seems to know why. Lashing out at members of other parties, races, or faiths is our way of releasing steam and deflecting attention from our own shortcomings.

Even if we manage to prevail over our adversaries, the only thing we have gained is power to continue to fail. We, too, can crash the plane.

So where does this leave us?

If society can recognize the hellish spiral of substance abuse, why do record numbers of people continue to put their health, careers, and relationships at risk? If we can acknowledge the corrosive effects of political and economic corruption, why do politicians, corporate policy makers, and grievance industries continue to thrive? If research statistics show that communities suffer grievous harm in the absence of judicial accountability, why do prosecutors and judges increasingly enable criminals to continue their reign of terror?

For many Christians the answer to these questions is straightforward. Secular society lacks the power to discern or overcome the consequences of sin because it has elected to follow a path that enthrones self over God. People are trapped because they either have not heard the gospel or have rejected it.

There is truth here—but there are also additional questions. For example, if social dysfunction is a feature of communities that have become gospel-free sanctuaries, then how do we explain why churches themselves continue to fracture like ice in the springtime? How can we call gospel followers *overcomers* when their schisms produce hurt and bitter people who proceed to deconstruct their faith? Why do 62 percent of evangelical men and 37 percent of senior pastors view pornography on a weekly basis?

It is common practice for people to be more censorious of others than they are of themselves. Today's activists freely accuse their Christian and conservative adversaries of being authoritarian fascists. It is far harder for them to acknowledge this same trait could be lurking in their own hearts and lives.

Professing Christians are no less blinded by their own hearts. This applies not only to their perspective on secular society, but also in the way they view their fellow believers. This is readily seen in a proliferation of censorious, heresy-hunting podcasters who publicly denounce the perceived shortcomings of other ministers—all while failing to recognize their own pride, slander, or lack of charity. Whose sin is greater?

According to Jesus, it is always wise to remove the plank from our own eyes before we say anything about the speck that obscures our brother's vision. Humility is a critical aspect of gospel truth, and it was this recognition that led David to petition God to examine his heart to see if there was any wicked way in him. Self-blindness can be deadly.

In a broader take on the root challenges facing secular society and the church, Jesus identifies three primary antagonists: the world, sin, and the devil.

Though society is largely oblivious to these threats (or discounts their relevancy), the church typically maintains an active stance against the world and sin. Although this stance has eroded somewhat as Christians have traded distinctiveness for accommodation, or even adoption, of worldly postures and practices, sin is still viewed as something that calls for avoidance or forgiveness.

The biggest convergence between the church and the world is found in the former's ignorance and dismissiveness of the devil's role in daily life. This is manifest both in the paucity of biblically based teaching on the subject, and in the measure of embarrassment or hesitancy that often accompanies conversations about the demonic.

This is unfortunate given the expanded number of openings extended to the enemy through occult media, pornography, sexual experimentation, and drug use. There is also evidence of increased demonic activity associated with humanity's proximity to the end of the age.

It is in this critical context that we welcome Heather Tayloe's timely book, *The Saboteur*. While not the first book to have been written on the subject, it is certainly among the more practical and comprehensive.

Of particular value is the book's unmasking of a being that has long pursued his tradecraft in anonymity. As any sports, business, political, or military strategist will attest, an offensive force achieves maximum impact when and where it is least suspected.

The devil's malign involvement in community and church life cannot be overestimated. It is real, it is ubiquitous, and it is growing. Those who diminish his role do so at their own peril.

As the apostle Paul wrote in his epistle to the Ephesians,

> We do not wrestle against flesh and blood, but against the rulers, against the authorities, against the cosmic powers over this present darkness, against the spiritual forces of evil in the heavenly places. (6:12 ESV)

If we are to make any sense of the turmoil and temptations that beset our world today, we must acknowledge these dark spiritual forces. The fact they are spiritual does not make them less real—*it makes them more real.* As spiritual beings ourselves, we are inextricably linked to the cosmic struggle that is being waged daily in a dimension that defines all that we are and all that we do.

To be ignorant of this dimension, or to make light of it, is to be condemned to a life defined by loose ends. On this treadmill of defeat, nothing makes sense and nothing gets solved. Ever.

As Heather points out, the enemy is a dirty and deceptive fighter with malign intent. His thieving mission, as defined by Jesus in John 10:10, is to "steal and kill and destroy" that which is precious to God. As human beings with the very breath of God in our lungs, we are positioned at the very top of heaven's list of valuables. And this makes us a prime target.

In addition to its extensive set of definitions and warnings, the book you now hold in your hands also offers thoroughly biblical remedies—for men, for women, for church leaders. These remedies include finding our identity and purpose, taking steps to protect our minds and families, and learning to walk in godly contentment.

The Saboteur has been on Heather's heart for many years now, and I am delighted it has finally taken form. It is good and timely seed, and it will strengthen you for the battles ahead.

George Otis, Jr.
Pleasant Hill, Missouri

Preface

No book *could* ever be an all-encompassing exposé on the dreadful exploits of satan and his dark workers. Nevertheless, there are many good books that have been written by those especially called to expose the devil, so if after finishing this one you want an even deeper understanding, check out Derek Prince's many books on this topic or George Otis Jr.'s, *The Twilight Labyrinth.* They're a good place to start. I see this as a stepstool to those other works once you've cut your teeth here.

> So then, let us not be like others, who are asleep, but *let us be awake and sober.* (1 Thessalonians 5:6 NIV)

Let's prepare by digging deep into the Lord. *Study and know* the Holy One, the King of Kings and Lord of Lords, the Lord of Hosts, the One described as the King who is coming soon, the Lord of Heaven's Armies who possesses a kingdom far greater and utterly unlike *any* creation that ever existed on earth or in heaven! Begin with Him! He knows the way and has the wisdom we need in this war.

This book could be a catalyst for genuine change in an *unexplained but very real area of powerlessness* in your life. It will impact your family, your business, and any other meaningful spiritual dynamic. On a larger scale, it provides helpful and timely insights into what appears to be the unstoppable and continuing regression of our society and culture on every level.

As God's representatives here on earth, we must deal with this very real enemy whether we wish to do so or not. Jesus candidly taught us about satan on multiple occasions, using many different names for him, so that we would be informed. We cannot blink him away as we did the boogeyman in our childhood dreams. Jesus was preparing His followers to stand because He understood what was going to happen next.

While my father was writing his book about a "lion who devours," I was a willing and ready sponge at his side. That man, whom I can gratefully claim as my father, and that book, which he penned so urgently with his fiery, eager mind, was used greatly to inform a spiritually hungry generation about their very real and very committed foe—one who would not be dissuaded from his never-ending attacks against them. This book, like my father's before me, was written to oust the unrelentingly evil saboteur once more, in my generation and for the generations to come.

Introduction

Are you awake? This book is a *warning*—one that is incredibly urgent! A long overdue trumpet blast is sounding right now, and it is for everyone. Even you. The enemy is working ruthlessly and determinedly to undermine the work of Jesus, and this is an urgent call from the Holy Spirit to get prepared and actively fight against the devil.

We are God's watchmen, and we have a grave responsibility to stand strong in Him and warn those around us of the danger ahead. We must not be silent!

> But if the watchman sees the sword coming and does not blow the trumpet, and the people are not warned, and the sword comes and takes any person from among them, he is taken away in his iniquity; but his blood I will require at the watchman's hand. (Ezekiel 33:6)

If there is no warning, there is ignorance, and because of that ignorance, people perish.

> Come, wild animals of the field! Come, wild animals of the forest! Come and devour my people! For the leaders of my people—the Lord's watchmen, his shepherds—are blind and ignorant. They are like silent watchdogs that give no warning when danger comes. They love to lie around, sleeping and dreaming. Like greedy dogs,

they are never satisfied. They are ignorant shepherds, all following their own path and intent on personal gain. "Come," they say, "let's get some wine and have a party. Let's all get drunk. Then tomorrow we'll do it again and have an even bigger party!" (Isaiah 56:9-12 NLT)

This passage paints a chilling picture of sheep with no protection. While the words frame the attitudes of the worthless shepherds, they also highlight the inherent danger we are facing today.

Perilous Days

Those situations in Ezekiel and Isaiah are not pleasant by any means, but we must heed and consider them. If we do not, the results will be tragic: We will be caught off guard by what we do not understand and miss what we should have done—or worse.

The peril of this situation is so great that we must recognize it and respond correctly. We must humble ourselves before the Lord and ask Him to teach us about spiritual warfare and our place in it. We have no time to waste. This book will help you do this.

Our enemy is dangerous. Who is he exactly, and what is he up to? First and foremost, the devil is a saboteur, which is one who engages in sabotage. The word *sabotage* reminds us of what happens during war when there is destruction of property or blocking normal operations, carried out to damage, destroy, or hinder a cause or activity. It is an intentional act of war, and saboteurs are enemy agents. They are also called the underground resistance.

These groups work deliberately and methodically to damage any activity of those they consider a target. Every shred of their being is dedicated to injuring and destroying their enemy.

The devil and his forces actively seek *to pull down* Jesus, His cause, and His people—plus anything the enemy has identified as at odds with his own fundamental plan of malice and evil.

In *Releasing Heaven on Earth, God's Principles for Releasing the Land*, Alistair P. Petrie wrote:

> A Christian steward is responsible for God's property. So long as we live in a world estranged from God, however, our stewardship is subject to defilement and therefore requires cleansing. Until this takes place, rocks, birds and thorns—the enemies of the seed in Jesus' parable—block people from entering the land God has prepared for them...a steward is called to reclaim for God the land that is rightfully His, which has been lost through fallen or sinful stewardship. It is our personal and corporate stewardship that gives access to satan, or that opens up the hearts and lives of people to God.[1]

> For *we do not* wrestle against flesh and blood, but against principalities, against powers, against the rulers of the darkness of this age, against spiritual hosts of wickedness *in the heavenly places*. (Ephesians 6:12)

When spiritually provoked, a large majority of people—inside and outside the church—are under the impression that whatever happened came about through flesh and blood—through people.

Let's press in on this one point. The truth is that people often dismissively explain away very real and active malevolent forces! These forces work in those who are aware as well as those who are not aware of satan's tactical maneuvers.

In fact, the scripture above has become overused and wrongly applied to an appalling degree. Thankfully though, these words weren't just written through the apostle Paul's scholarly expertise and training; they were written *under the influence of God's Holy Spirit,* so these words will forever be incredibly effective because of God's promise attached to them.

---

1. Alistair P. Petrie, *Releasing Heaven on Earth, God's Principles for Releasing the Land* (Baker Publishing Group, 2000), 49.

> So shall My word be that goes forth from My mouth; it shall not return to Me void, but *it shall accomplish* what I please, and *it shall prosper* in the thing for which I sent it. (Isaiah 55:11)

What's Really Going On Here?

But let's back this up for a moment. The whole of Isaiah 55 is incredible, so study it when you can, but Isaiah 55:7 (NIV) says, "Let the wicked forsake their ways and the unrighteous their thoughts."

Let's apply what is being considered here regarding God's will and His Word. The truth is that every day, we run up against very real darkness; it is hate-filled and hate-driven. God's Word is not unaware of this supernatural battle that is being played out inside, but above, the natural realm. These evil forces have unique power that is beyond the human realm, and they are commanded by the evil one, the saboteur. In their essence, they have a dark spirit form and are filled with malicious, malevolent, and destructive intent all the time. They exist! They are beyond redemption, they are ruthless, and they are relentless.

For some, that is a shocking revelation. Others give it a ho-hum shrug as if it's not a big deal. A ho-hum attitude about the devil and his wicked cohorts should *never* be embraced within the body of Christ! Never! Jesus Himself said we were to *be wary,* so why should we consider this demonic and shadowy activity to be less serious than we would a flesh-and-blood enemy we could see?

These dark forces *will never stop* doing what they do—working evil incessantly, fleshing out every plan instigated by dark enemy agents under their chief false shepherd, satan himself. They will never stop until they are forced to do so by the return of Jesus, which is manifestly evident and soon!

A Mature Understanding

The body of Christ should not be so ridiculously immature about the devil's tactics, as though we are unaware of the presence of these forces in the world. We need to face the truth. We cannot shrug off the fact that enemy agents can—and do—get into our churches and make a mess of them to a terrible extent. They should not be able to do this! Nevertheless, they do get away with it, and it's because there is terrible misunderstanding and ignorance in the body due to a lack of biblical instruction about the saboteur's specific work. Satan's supreme delight is to hobble Christians of all shapes and creeds—*wherever* he finds them, period.

If we cease to teach that the devil is real, his supernatural antics gain supremacy *from the pulpits*—not because he is supreme, but because we've made the mistake of discounting him entirely, thereby giving him plenty of latitude to do what he wants. We have already seen this publicly displayed in churches to a gross degree. We decided the devil was ineffectual against believers and left it at that. The lack of biblical savvy *inside* the church is evidenced everywhere as some leadership has, in many locales, discounted the devil as not even *existing*. Worse still, many have welcomed him into the church by *mixing* the gospel of Christ with beliefs contrary to it, teaching that both could co-exist: the gospel of a crucified Savior alongside the worship of another "god." "Anything goes," they preach.

But it doesn't work like that.

> Now the Spirit expressly says that in latter times some will depart from the faith, giving heed to deceiving spirits and doctrines of demons. (1 Timothy 4:1)

The old adage that doing nothing is actually engaging and *sanctioning something* (my personal paraphrase) is absolutely true! Doing nothing is, in fact, making a choice to *do* nothing, but it does not follow that nothing is happening as a result of our inaction. Oh, my beloved friend, something *is* happening. The fact that many believe this subject doesn't matter is evidence of our lack of teaching and training, and it is unconscionable. Let's get back to brass tacks!

Satan's Work

God is God, and satan is a rebellious, fallen angel. He held a high position in heaven and was designed by the Creator as something like an archangel. That is not a supernatural position to be sniffed at! But it all changed when he chose evil. Today, he no longer holds that position, and he is not like God in any way whatsoever.

Satan is not supreme like God in any way, shape, or form. Whatever he does is pretense. Whatever he does is projection. Whatever he does is manipulation. He lives to lead everyone in the polar opposite direction of the one in which God, through the Holy Spirit, desires to lead them.

However, and please hear me, precious reader, none of those facts render him or his wicked underlings devoid of power. Even though he is a defeated foe in the end, and we all know that he is, we cannot discount him or his agents. It is foolish—and dangerous—to assume we do not have to know anything about him now, because right now, he is actively operating as the prowling and hungry beast he is. He is described in the Word as a *hungry* lion. This descriptor fits its purpose: We need to know exactly what we are dealing with, and further, recognize that we are dealing with him *all* the time. His hunger for death and destruction will be never satisfied until he is destroyed by the Son of God in the lake of fire.[2] An actual lion is satisfied after feeding. The saboteur is *never* satisfied, so do not kid yourself into thinking he has relented in his pursuit of you. He will never stop hunting you. You must be vigilant at all times—he is.

We Are in a Battle

Let me interject something pertinent to our discussion before we move on. Though Jesus's work on the cross was a thorough work, leaving nothing on the table, satan (as an extant being) carries on ruthlessly and will not be destroyed until the end. His end will be according to Jesus's timing and not his own. Jesus died "once and for all," saying at His death, "It is finished."[3] Understand then that there is no unfinished business as

---

2. See Revelation 20:10.
3. See John 19:30.

far as Christ's utter defeat of satan. The first death is the physical death, while the second is eternal death, or eternal separation from God. This is a question of our eternal destiny. It's that serious. Our culture has made a mockery of this, as though it is a joke, writing songs about wishing we could be in hell but scoffing at the idea completely.

Jesus took a different approach. He understood the danger we were in and absolutely destroyed the work of the devil on the cross. He made a way for us to be part of His family.

That means the devil is an eternal being awaiting his dreadful and eternal judgment from the Lord right now. Believe me, the devil is happy when people decide he does not exist. Meanwhile, he tears, wounds, or takes down all those he can grab using his effective toolbox of demonic life hacks. These are the means he has successfully been using for centuries. So don't be fooled by him. He is the chief of deceivers! He's very sneaky. You *thought* that accepting *little bites* of his dark substance into your life wouldn't place *you* into his boat headed across the River Styx and straight into hell, but think again. You would be wrong about that. That's why this study is vital to every person alive now. We are in a battle, and every choice we make matters.

> The LORD is my rock, my fortress and my deliverer; my God is my rock, in whom I take refuge, my shield and the horn of my salvation, my stronghold. (Psalm 18:2 NIV)

Chapter 1

Early Training: Basic Training

From the time we were small, my father intentionally taught us about the spiritual enemy of our soul. I am the youngest of four children. Additionally, my mother taught me to find evidence of the enemy's ways from God's Word and how to sincerely love and honor the Bible and its Author, the Holy Spirit. They also modeled lives of fearing God above all and trusting to the earnestness of prayer for insight over anything else.

I learned to mine the Bible, God's holy Word. My parents modeled these foundational disciplines by pointing out how the gentle prodding of the precious Holy Spirit worked in their own lives! The gratitude I feel for that unusual gift of both parents' nurture in this way is unbounded! As I've raised my own family and mentored others, I have been greatly indebted to my godly upbringing. It has produced rich and meaningful fruit in my life and touched so many others.

My father had a driving curiosity about God's will and His ways, which registered in his bright, earnest, sparklingly clear blue eyes. To say he was a firecracker of a man—dynamic, authentic, inspirational, and larger-than-life in all the best ways—is absolutely true. Although he was a self-made and successful man, his most prolific years truly began when God got a hold of him. Soon after, my father was powerfully baptized in the Holy Spirit, which placed a meaningful and life-altering grip on his life. His spiritually fruitful years began in his late forties. It was during this time period that I was born.

It is never too soon to begin training a young child in God's ways. My parents are an excellent example of the wisdom of this. They took their position as parents and guardians of their children very seriously from the time we were very young. While remaining age-appropriate, they did not leave us uninformed about the warfare we would face in this world. They championed God's ways far more than the devil's, so we grew up with a clear understanding of God's supremacy in all things.

I mention this because many parents believe the very young to be incapable of grasping such knowledge and decide, wrongly, to leave that subject up to time and chance. In doing so, they abdicate their God-given and honored parental role, and by default allow others to "parent" their children. However, those children were entrusted to them by God.

This is an enormous mistake, especially in this hour! It doesn't matter whether that esteemed position has been surrendered to a church, school, coach, or something else entirely. A lack of parenting will bear terrible fruit. Lives are ruined due to the lack of parental instruction in the home—and yes, even at a very young age.

The saboteur is active in any area in which you give him space. He's prowling in your gaps and lapses! He's not taking a nap! It is vital that our children be guided in the full counsel of the Lord by fully engaged parents and guardians (grandparents and more). Children (of any age) should not be left wholly unequipped for what they are sure to meet in this life!

Most sensible people would find the idea of going boating without a life jacket just plain stupid. Knowing the inherent dangers involved, why take such a chance? In the same way, we don't start playing a sport without understanding it and maybe finding a coach. With the benefit of both, we slowly learn how to play. This is true of any undertaking. With the necessary coaching and instruction, we play soccer, dance, draw, or master an instrument. Along the way, we will experience some bumps and bruises as we grow in the necessary know-how. You'd never throw a first-time boxer into the ring with a heavyweight champion!

Just like that boxer, our precious children must be raised with the understanding and coaching they need to successfully deal with their enemy. A caregiver should never send their sacred charge into the spiritual fray without the slightest mention of the unseen forces lying in wait for them there. The saboteur and his deadly agents are vicious, and if we do not take our place, but turn a blind eye, it will be disastrous for our children.

My parents were faithful to identify the true culprit behind the global and personal pain and confusion so easily traced through history since the cradle of time. They did not under-inform me about the devil and what he did, but at the same time, they were sure to give God, the character of God, prayer, and His Word its proper position in my young heart and mind.

One of the reasons some parents choose not to teach their young children, or pre-teens, about the devil is because they think that talking about it will stir up unnecessary fear or angst. I've also been told, repeatedly, that somehow giving the devil more airtime than God is not necessary since they (or their child) are a believer. This is invariably followed by this verse: "The one who is in you is powerful. He is more powerful than the one who is in the world" (1 John 4:4b NIRV).

These parents have decided that the saboteur isn't that real to them. This shows they have not taken the time to see who the Bible says he is, including the words of Jesus in John 8, Matthew 13 and 25, and Luke 4. They use this verse as an excuse instead of allowing that they are foolishly making their own private peace with the subject without actually understanding it at all. Ignorance is not bliss.

For decades, I have heard this type of scenario. Though I felt disappointed after these encounters, I did not immediately recognize how widespread this serious problem was *inside* the church. It has led to impotency in the body of Christ when true power was needed. Treating the enemy as nonexistent has left an open playing field, allowing him to wreak havoc because no spiritual weaponry has been raised against him. Meanwhile, the Bible relates quite a bit about the dark forces in the world:

> One day the evil spirit answered them, "Jesus I know, and Paul I know about, but who are you?" Then the man who had the evil spirit jumped on them and overpowered them all. He gave them such a beating that they ran out of the house naked and bleeding. (Acts 19:15-16 NIV)

> You believe that there is one God. Good! Even the demons believe that—and shudder. (James 2:19 NIV)

Do we read these sections of the Bible and think, *Well now, that's a truly uncomfortable story. I'm not going to teach or talk about that again.* Let's look at this in another context. Luke relates this situation when these guys ignorantly tried cast out an evil spirit. They tried to wield the power of Jesus without really believing in Him and, instead, ran head-on into the adversary's trap, escaping injured and afraid. We should not make the same mistake.

> They are a nation without sense, there is no discernment in them. If only they were wise and would understand this and discern what their end will be! (Deuteronomy 32:28-29 NIV)

Enlightenment is there for those who treat God's Word correctly: as the one truth without which they cannot live. Nevertheless, if this subject continues to be taught with yawning ignorance, even those who seek God will be led down another path entirely. Sin and other gods crouch at our door continuously, begging admittance into our heart and mind. Let's learn to recognize these things so we can combat them from a place of divine understanding, wisdom, power, and authority!

Not giving *any* useful teaching or spiritual training of this nature, including even cursory teaching and helpful definitions, to children, particularly when they are young, has had an absolutely devastating effect on the current generation. The fruit of this is obvious. They can pick up all kinds of occult know-how through social media, their friends, early sexual encounters, gaming (especially immersive gaming), yoga, New Age practices, and so much more. There are even outlets posing as environmentally friendly and offering rituals, incantations, music, books, movies, TV programs—as many possibilities as you have the imagination to support! It all exists to distract and woo people away from the One who rightfully deserves all of their attention.

The Word of God must be first and foremost; it is our foundation for life.

We are witnessing everywhere the unspeakable tragedy of the failure of the wider family of believers not doing the work in this area that Jesus outlined for His disciples. It is time to pick up the mantle and begin teaching His Word again. We must lay aside all other gospels that vie for supremacy over Jesus's gospel. In the same way, we must reject books and teachings—no matter how well-written or recommended they may be—that do not line up with the Word of God. The Word of God must be first and foremost; it is our foundation for life.

We must carry His witness from our mouth to those who do not know or understand the true gospel. However, to those who have faithfully educated and fought this very real fight, thank you, well done, and God bless you!

The concept of a real saboteur is not new. The Word of God has plenty to say about it. The Word is full of light, wisdom, and understanding. It is an absolute blessing for those who will take the time to study and keep in step with its expert guidance. This makes it unique and unlike any other book.

The Bible has been instructing generations of believers (and non-believers too) on how to live, what to expect, and what has gone before them. It is the most vital spiritual record ever to be written. It has always been a bestseller! It is there for us, faithfully waiting to be picked up, read, loved, and cherished—but too few bother to pick it up now.

People read and listen to anything and everything else quite avidly but tend to leave the Bible on the shelf, where it gathers dust. Let's be real: Though the Bible should be the most-read book, we've allowed our culture to dictate its own thoughts about God's Word as the hour grows darker, just as Jesus said would happen![4]

The Bible does not claim to entertain, but it is the sword the New Testament says it is. We cannot afford to leave it on the shelf. We do not have to remain in darkness. That shows both ignorance of sin as well as ignorance of our spiritual foe. Colossians tells us this:

> For he has rescued us from the dominion of darkness
> and brought us into the kingdom of the Son he loves,
> in whom we have redemption, the forgiveness of sins.
> (Colossians 1:13-14 NIV)

Jesus is the one true King, and He will return! We must be ready when He comes.

> It will be good for those servants whose master finds
> them ready, even if he comes in the middle of the night
> or toward daybreak. (Luke 12:38 NIV)

If you don't know Him while reading this book, it's my sincere hope that before finishing it, you will! Jesus said this:

> Blessed are those who hunger and thirst for righteousness,
> for they will be filled. (Matthew 5:6 NIV)

Be a seeker! Be curious and ask God your questions in prayer. He will answer!

---

4. See John 3:19.

For the word of God is living and powerful, and sharper than any two-edged sword, piercing even to the division of soul and spirit, and of joints and marrow, and is a discerner of the thoughts and intents of the heart. (Hebrews 4:12)

Father, I pray for every precious reader to know You and to experience Your great love as You take them through these pages. I pray that they would know Jesus as their Savior and Lord and connect with the Holy Spirit in such a powerful way that they would be led by Him all the days of their life here on this earth, until You bring them to their eternal home with You. I pray they will know and fulfill the powerful call You have placed on their life. In Jesus's Name. Amen.

Chapter 2

Exactly Who Is the Saboteur?

As God's stewards, we make sure our spiritual antennae are fine tuned to His perception of life and reality.[5]
—Alistair Petrie

There are reasons why my first book out of the gate is this one. The Holy Spirit's strong promptings no longer seemed gentle but had become urgent. Those who know Him know that He moves very distinctly. I also saw a pattern in my life that unveiled a mission to wake up my fellow travelers—those who know Jesus and those who do not—to the reality of the saboteur's existence, as that certainty has ebbed significantly in the body of Christ. Everyone needs to understand that his plan is evil and malevolent in nature, and it is daily directed at men, women, and children everywhere.

Just in my lifetime alone, there has been a shockingly dangerous drift from even speaking about his damaging work inside and outside of the church—to our own hurt. By and large, we've pushed him out of our mind and rendered him a "notion" of sorts, a phantasmic dark figure of movies, campfire lore, and macabre Hollywood storytelling. While the occasional ghost story will certainly give us chills, there are strong

5. Alistair Petrie, *Releasing Heaven on Earth*, (Ada, Michigan: Chosen Books, 2000), 56.

suggestions that the devil is fictional. In the Western world, people laugh at the mere idea that the devil is real.

That's not how it is in the spiritual hot zones of the globe though. These areas deal with perpetual warfare, corruption, and chaos. These places live in sin, such as prostitution, generational witchcraft practices, drug abuse, usury, greed, and more. In these spots, you will find every criminal thing, natural and supernatural, opposing God's plans and God's ways. But the saboteur's work is not relegated just to those obvious areas of darkness. You may be surprised, but he lurks in every neighborhood on earth through sin. He is welcomed (or summoned) through a variety of sins or direct occult practices.

The saboteur is both more and less than the ghost stories and red-pajama-wearing, clip-on-horns figure often portrayed during holiday romps and evident in every culture and nation on earth. He wraps himself in lies, so there are many around the world who believe he is real but also believe him to somehow be their friend. They do not see him for who he really is. They don't understand that he will use them as he destroys them, seeking their death apart from God most of all.

Through seemingly casual, friendly encounters, this group of people believes they can consume horror or paranormal movies at a clip, without any damage to their soul. These are also those who say Halloween or the solstices are their favorite holiday. In fact, we are living in an age in which very young children are being targeted with occult ideas in cartoons, games, toys, etc. They routinely open the computer gaming portal (a door) and have access to occult books, manga, anime, as well as pornography of every kind. Children and young adults are reading books with similar themes with frequency and delight.

Many people have no problem engaging in psychic readings or participating in occult encounters. You'll find them dabbling with tarot cards, playfully interacting with a Ouija board, being entertained by palm reading, or visiting mediums who can channel familiar spirits, which they are urged to call their "friend."

Lots of people rely on astrological charts to influence their personal decisions according to their sign. Often, occult pursuits are done under the guise of finding good health. Yoga and New Age practices teach followers to chant the names of demons—knowingly or unknowingly inviting their entrance into their body. They shrug this off as though it were nothing, even though they just opened themselves up to harm. Although these are just doorways, they are designed to ultimately lead you into darker alleyways of the occult to bring about your destruction.

> Do not turn to mediums or seek out spiritists, for you will be defiled by them. I am the LORD your God. (Leviticus 19:31 NIV)

> When someone tells you to consult mediums and spiritists, who whisper and mutter, should not a people inquire of their God? Why consult the dead on behalf of the living? (Isaiah 8:19 NIV)

This is but a short laundry list of the multiple avenues of deception the enemy uses to ensnare us. These false-power, false-healing, false-knowledge propositions are not new to him. It is time we made a break with him and become fully awake to the facts about who he is and what he does.

The saboteur delights in being talked about and highlighted and feared.

The saboteur delights in being talked about and highlighted and feared. The more "play" he can get, the better. He thinks it takes away or somehow takes a bite out of the attention that should go to the Most High. To that, I scoff wholeheartedly. Nothing can diminish the character of the living, active, loving, sacrificing, creative, and mighty beyond all knowing God! He is my King! The saboteur is universally out of the Most High God's league!

This book has zero to do with elevating his status one iota! The goal is simply to expose his tactics so his unending plays on your life will be laid bare.

Regrettably, the Christian church has largely altered its stance about how we teach about the devil. Now in a critical stage of ignorance, the church is no longer effective against his onslaughts. This has resulted in catastrophe: An entire group of believers in Jesus are not feeding regularly on the Word's knowledge for themselves, and they are subsequently "open game" for the devil. Those inside the church are undereducated and critically uninformed. Therefore, at the leading of the Holy Spirit, it is time to train Jesus's church, reminding them once again that they are not dealing with something fake.

There is a significant threat at work: one that is harmful, dark, wicked, deceptive, and a supernatural force with many schemes. God is greater, but it is vital that we acknowledge the devil's existence and receive fundamental training about how to deal with this wily, dangerous, antagonistic, and aggressive foe. He is set on keeping us reeling in misery, shame, hatred, abuse, confusion, self-harm, sexual impurity and perversion, adultery, unforgiveness, pain, self-hatred, suicide, addiction, depression, grief, and loss. He wants us lost in a haze of doubt, swimming in false ideologies. "Pick your poison" is the phrase the devil poses.

If this wasn't enough, he wants people in that state the whole time, even while he robs them, cheats them, lies to them, and uses them in the most heinous and insidious ways he can devise. He expertly and manipulatively herds them on their way to hell with him. And yes, that is a real place.

It only took a few generations for the enemy to make sure that most church folks don't believe him to be real. In that condition, as my mom used to say, all kinds of shenanigans ensue. But this isn't cute. Fast-paced or slow-moving, the saboteur's ways are deadly, horrific, and traumatizing, as he brings about as much overall destruction as he can. The truth is that even though many horrible events are credited to other causes, he is at the root of them.

> The thief does not come except to steal, and to kill, and
> to destroy. I have come that they may have life, and that
> they may have it more abundantly. (John 10:10)

Jesus told His disciples in the hours before his own death on a Roman cross:

> Watch and pray, lest you enter into temptation. The spirit
> indeed is willing, but the flesh is weak. (Matthew 26:41)

The devil is the tempter, and weakened flesh is his specialty, as you will learn. I am not suggesting, dear reader, that all poor decisions, difficulties, or tragedies are instigated by him, but Jesus said he had a role to play in this world and that we were not to consider him stupid (my words).

> Be alert and of sober mind. Your enemy the devil prowls
> around like a roaring lion looking for someone to devour.
> Resist him, standing firm in the faith, because you know that
> the family of believers throughout the world is undergoing
> the same kind of sufferings. (1 Peter 5:8-9 NIV)

Some think that if you ignore him, he'll just go away, or worse, they stop teaching about him altogether because the subject matter makes modern churchgoers uneasy in their seats.

Jesus used the word "crafty" when describing the devil, so if you did not already consider him a real challenger to your faith-life, and you are looking to grow, you can expect opposition! Jesus made it clear that even though you may be facing flesh and blood (other people), they can be "puppeteered" by the saboteur's agents, which are not flesh and blood by nature.

If you have never read C.S. Lewis's *The Screwtape Letters*, check it out. It is eye-opening in this area. Again, to make myself perfectly clear, the devil is not a contender to Jesus; Jesus is the One, the only Christ, and the very heart of the gospel message!

Meanwhile, the tempter is bent on destruction. He will do absolutely anything to keep people from being saved. He doesn't want us to be loving, knowing, serving, and telling others about Jesus, so he'll do anything possible to prevent that. Thankfully, God's Word contains what we need to recognize his playbook and avoid his age-old pitfalls. He is an expert at what he does, but not one of his moves is new. Everything he does is old hat.

He does not, nor has he ever, played fair. Don't ever expect that from him.

It should be noted that the devil is not someone you can "date" while also saying that you love Jesus and consider Him (Jesus) your Savior. The saboteur is not a pocket pal; he will not stay in his pocket or his lane—ever! So if you are dabbling, toying, or in any way participating in the occult, stop! It will lead to your demise, no matter how little it is. Stop it now! The devil is real, and his sabotage has dragged many down, delivering them to judgment. Hell is described as a lake of fire that is reserved particularly for him and his demons. We have no time for foolishness. We have work to do!

Who Is This Saboteur?

The devil is a wholly rebellious being. Often called "the fallen one," he hates God more than you or I could ever imagine. Satan desperately wanted—and still wants—to *be God*. This is an impossibility. He wants more than anything else the worship that is due only to God, and he will try to his last breath to get it in any way he can. He does not, nor has he ever, played fair. Don't ever expect that from him. There is only one Savior, and it is not the devil. In his pride, satan led his fellow rebellious supernatural beings in a mass revolt against God. Each of them made their own choice willingly and according to their own free will. They are fallen, which means they are disconnected from the full power and insight of God. Because they are disconnected from the One who made them (by their own choice), and now await eternal damnation, they are rebellious, angry, and stateless, supernatural beings. Satan is a rejected, deceptive, murdering liar, a fraudster of the worst order, stirring up as much woe as possible, especially to those who bear the image of the One (Jesus) whom the devil aches to be, but can never, ever be!

Satan's beginning (before his entry to earth) is found in the book of Isaiah:

> How you have fallen from heaven,
> morning star [KJV, "O Lucifer"], son of the dawn!
> [Bright One of the Dawn, Day Star, Lucifer]
> You have been cast down to the earth,
> you who once laid low the nations!
> You said in your heart,
> "I will ascend to the heavens;
> I will raise my throne
> above the stars of God;
> I will sit enthroned on the mount of assembly,
> on the utmost heights of Mount Zaphon.
> I will ascend above the tops of the clouds;
> I will make myself like the Most High."
> But you are brought down to the realm of the dead,
> to the depths of the pit.
> (Isaiah 14:12-15 NIV)

Take note of all those "I will" statements! The truth is that he was unable to do *any* of those things at the time and will never be able to do them in the future either.

> For by Him all things were created that are in heaven and that are on earth, visible and invisible, whether thrones or dominions or principalities (rulers) or powers

(authorities). All things were created through Him and for Him. (Colossians 1:16)

The bottom line here is simple; the devil is just a cosmic poser! Real power and authority have always existed and will always exist with God. Period.

Real power and authority have always existed and will always exist with God.

In Luke, we read that Jesus sends out seventy-two witnesses in pairs to talk about the kingdom of God. They returned to talk with Jesus about their experiences. Let's read a little here:

> "Whoever listens to you listens to me [Jesus]; whoever rejects you rejects me; but whoever rejects me rejects him who sent me [God the Father]." The seventy-two returned with joy and said, "Lord, even the demons submit to us in your name." (Luke 10:16-17 NIV)

Clearly, Jesus wanted His witnesses to be encouraged in their ministry for Him because they were assured of the place He had reserved for them in His eternal kingdom, rather than because of the power that flowed mightily through them. In recognizing that, let's not in the next breath diminish that Jesus also made it abundantly clear that demonic spirits were real. And further, He expects us, as those laboring in His kingdom work, to help those in that kind of bondage so they can be set free from the devil's grip!

Overcoming *all* the power of the enemy is the core of Jesus's redemptive work! You cannot walk with Jesus through the pages of His Word and find any other agenda. Jesus's every move was rooted in obediently flowing in His lavish love, one that is so great that you can spend a lifetime plumbing it and barely skim its beauty. Jesus is all about unshackling anyone who is bound in the traps, devices, schemes, and evil planned for them by satan. Jesus's goal is to free His human creation made in His likeness. Jesus delights in filling His "jars of clay" (that's us) to full measure with the treasure of His Holy Spirit!

> And having disarmed the powers and authorities, he
> made a public spectacle of them, triumphing over them
> by the cross. (Colossians 2:15 NIV)

Jesus died so that we could walk in victory and overturn the enemy's plots. We are birthed into His kingdom and filled with His Spirit, so we are equipped for this battle.

Chapter 3

Doubt Drudger

The devil will always work to change the temperature setting of the water coming out of your spigot until it's more to his *liking*.

In his starring, debut role, he came upon the scene of time, not as a fictional character from some old book, but full of malice and wrath. At that time, he did not slither, but we do meet him in the perfection of the garden of Eden, where the two newly created human beings lived. One had been made from the flesh of the other, the woman from the man, and both possessed God's utterly divine spark, the *ruach*, or breath of life. There they met him, and he was simply called "the serpent."

Here is what is said of him directly:

> Now the serpent was *more crafty* than any of the wild animals the LORD God had made. (Genesis 3:1 NIV)

Here's how different Bible versions have translated this word: *The Orthodox Jewish Bible* tells us the serpent was more "cunning, crafty, wiley"[6] while the *King James Version* uses the word "subtle," and the *New Living Translation* refers to him as "the shrewdest of the wild animals."

---

6. See *The Orthodox Jewish Bible* fourth edition, OJB. Copyright 2002,2003,2008,2010, 2011 by Artists for Israel International. All rights reserved.

When the lights come up on this scene, Adam and Eve, male and female, the very best of God's perfect creation, stand fresh, pure, and untouched by any sin. What does this cunning and shrewd being say to God's image-bearers (the first humans) who had the breath of God in them? Replying to Eve's explanation that there was a tree called the Tree of Knowledge of Good and Evil in the garden, from which they should not eat, he uttered these infamous words:

"Did God *really* say…?"

It was not unusual for Adam and Eve to speak to the animals, but the serpent went on to adjust God's words even further, while Adam stood nearby listening to the whole exchange. He was planting seeds of doubt. Satan is a drudger of doubts.

The devil will always work to change the temperature setting of the water coming out of your spigot until it's more to his liking.

However, he wasn't just questioning ideas between human beings; he was planting doubt about the words of God to His own creation. He was questioning God's command to Adam and his helper and wife, Eve.

He goes on: "You must not eat from *any* tree in the garden?"

> The LORD God took the man and put him in the Garden of Eden to work it and take care of it. And *the LORD God commanded* the man, "You are free to eat from any tree in the garden; but *you must not eat from the tree of the knowledge of good and evil*, for when you eat from it you will *certainly* die." (Genesis 2:15-17 NIV)

Oh, dear ones, God gave them all—but one.

Now let's go forward in Genesis and see what the devil does next:

> "You will not certainly die," the serpent said to the woman. "For God knows that when you eat from it your eyes will be opened, and *you will be like God, knowing good and evil.*" (Genesis 3:4-5 NIV)

There is so much going on in this one inglorious and tragically compelling suggestion to Eve, his every word dripping with evil.

To us, a speaking serpent (even one that probably had legs) seems like a fairytale, but for Adam and Eve, this was part of their daily work, a pleasurable marvel. This was a paradise of paradises! Adam worked with all parts of God's creation—naming them and speaking with God about them. I do not think the appearance of this creature was alarming to Adam or Eve. In fact, I think he was *dazzling,* as in Ezekiel 28:13! Neither of them would have had any previous knowledge of what this subtle creature was to introduce into their lives until they chose to disobey God. The repercussions going forward were much greater than they understood, although God had told them they would die.

The enemy took a cue from *the word-twist* regarding God's command to Adam, and then Adam to Eve:

> When the woman saw that the fruit of the tree was *good for food* and *pleasing to the eye,* and also *desirable for gaining wisdom,* she took some and ate it. She also gave some to her husband, who was with her, and he ate it. Then the eyes of both of them were opened, and they realized they were naked; so they sewed fig leaves together and made coverings for themselves. (Genesis 3:6-7 NIV)

In this short visit, the devil countermanded, lied, and blasphemed God. As a trust-bender, he sowed discord into perfection and purity, planting a false reality by painting a picture in their minds they did not already have—one that pointed away from God and made them think of themselves first. Selfish and self-centered thinking led to that first disobedient action against God. The devil speaking through the willing serpent made it sound like the fruit of the tree was a good thing—not only nourishing, but able to make one wise! He blemished God's character while speaking to God's own exquisite masterpiece. He tempted them to call God's character into question.

The doubt drudger made them believe God had withheld something from them that might make them like God. He was able to pull all this off, even making the newly created, pure human beings think it was really their idea, and perhaps dropping a hint or two that made it sound like it might even be something God would want for them. I mean, what could be so wrong about that?

But that's not how it worked out. The serpent instigated their fall. The devil's subtleties know no bounds; and if you do not see them here, you will not notice them in your everyday life. We don't want to fall for the same foul gags!

Doubt is a terrible blemish on the spiritual landscape of our relationship with God.

Stop and ask the Lord right now for His Holy Spirit discernment. May you not fall for the enemy's insertion of doubt in your mind and heart. Be aware that it is often sown during times of fear, woundedness, misunderstanding, and offense—times when our defenses have been breached in some way.

Doubt is a terrible blemish on the spiritual landscape of our relationship with God. Satan, that foul serpent, knows what he's doing full well. He's been there before. Let's talk about the heavenly rebellion.

Satan didn't just infect heaven with his insinuations of venomous pride and doubt. He, in the very first role he landed on earth, infected the first two perfect masterpieces of God's creation on earth. So unholy was he in his arrogant desire to overthrow heaven that he amassed an army against God and was, in the end, thrust by God and His angels from heaven's bright perfection. A third of heaven's host had followed him, and they were all swept to earth alongside him.

These evil and fallen beings were hurled to earth's pre-creation void along with the devil. There they began their usual rebellious, hateful labors! However, they no longer had any heavenly connection. It is exceedingly important that we understand this and not underestimate these forces. As supernatural beings, they do possess some serious talents for evil, but in some cases, we project far more power on these fallen supernatural beings than they deserve. Jesus's name, Jesus's blood, and our testimony about Jesus—along with the sword of the Spirit (God's Word spoken aloud)—overcome them absolutely! Some demons require us to be prayed up and fasting to dispatch them, but they have less authority than any man, woman, or child who is submitted to God, armed with the Word of God, and empowered by the Holy Spirit. We are equipped to deal with them!

You cannot, however, deal with anything, in any kind of authority, if you don't believe the devil exists or you don't believe he is a problem for you because you are a believer in Jesus Christ.

God does not appreciate or tolerate His Word being questioned. In Job 38:2, God says, "Who is this who darkens counsel by words without knowledge?"

You can then well imagine how angered God was by what the serpent had done in the garden. Let's look at what happened to the serpent because of what the saboteur had done, and the specific curse incurred:

> So the LORD God said to the serpent: "Because you have done this, you are cursed more than all cattle, and more than every beast of the field; on your belly you shall go, and you shall eat dust all the days of your life. And I will put enmity between you and the woman, and between your seed and her Seed; He shall bruise your head, and you shall bruise His heel." (Genesis 3:14-15)

Sowing doubt is one of the devil's more-worn suits in his closet of dragon wear! It sounds funny, but it's absolutely true. May the Holy Spirit reveal this truth to us, and may we grasp it.

This was the enemy's way *from the beginning*. He is still doing this now. He will snatch the very breath (the words) spoken between people to redirect and distract them, to sow discord and disunity. He plants seeds of discontent in every place he can, especially one that had once been pure. He lives to counter oneness with a question mark, like this: "Did God really say?" Can you see the collective furrowed brow that accompanies those words when they come from the mouth of God's creation everywhere? This is so his doing.

Sowing doubt is one of the devil's more-worn suits in his closet of dragon wear!

So be informed, the saboteur can't create the breath, but he can be sure to meddle in its intended operation. Let's stop and take this in. Satan will point to creation (us) and speak according to his own nature. Remember, he is a liar. He will plant his seeds: "Don't look at me; it was God's design flaw! It's God's fault that my life is so unhappy! He let that happen." Reread this until it sinks in! These thoughts are seeds of doubt.

Next, we accuse God—or one another—because we listened to that old serpent! After that, even though the pain we are in is completely the work of the devil, he tries to turn it on us further. He never stops, but relentlessly accuses God, spewing more lies into our brain. Meanwhile, God is good. Stay with me here. Even though God has not changed, all who listen to satan go on to blame God for the fault of the pain that came from it—instead of giving God the glory for whatever good was meant to come of His work through all things at all times. This change of focus has deadly consequences.

Please reread this section until you see it. Pray through it. Pray over yourself that you will have ears to hear, eyes to see, and a heart of understanding through the Holy Spirit. Watch for distractions that show up suddenly while you are reading this chapter. His ways are insidious.

Exposing the enemy's stratagems is painful, as they touch us and those around us, but we can trust Jesus to help us. A doctor never makes an incision and leaves the tender inner viscera exposed to germs. Instead, a physician cleans and dresses the wound and checks on it to make sure it heals correctly. That describes the work of the Holy Spirit. Additionally, a good physician will never leave any kind of identified corruption untouched. If we sincerely seek to be healed, evil must be addressed.

> This is the message which we have heard from Him and declare to you, that God is light and in Him is no darkness at all. (1 John 1:5)

This passage offers both the remedy and the prescription! The Holy Spirit displays Jesus in His every quality. He stands with us in this battle.

The saboteur does not operate creatively, but only deceptively and stealthily, cunningly and with malicious intent. He wants to ruin that which God meant for good. He will do this every time and as often as we allow. Tell him no! In Christ, we have the power to say, "No! I see you. I'm not going to do it your way, but God's way!" The enemy will continue sowing evil, working incessantly. His purpose is to sour your mind and heart, and destroy the marvelous, the beautiful, and the exquisite things of God. Though he can't create anything like God can, he will seek to distort the precious, the pure, the righteous, even the justice of what is good and godly.

The saboteur will twist the words from God to rip up what God wants to do through you! It's pure blasphemy, but he doesn't ever feel the need to play above board. He will even try to use Scripture in a corrupted way, as he did with Jesus after His long fast (Luke 4:2).

Do not let him manipulate either you or your neighbor's words or actions. Don't let him cause you to literally rip up God's dreams for you by the roots, tearing them out of the ground—undone and unfinished—or worse, to remake them in the distorted dmages of his mind instead, and call it God's work. It is like a spiritual abortion or stillbirth. The golden calf is an cxample of this in Exodus 32:1.

How many times have you looked at the wreckage, the effects of the devil's work, in a person's dream that God had created good? That dream had been given by God and for His glory, and it was supposed to be accomplished in joy, but the saboteur arrived and stole it. The proverbial rug has been pulled right out from under us through any number of schemes, while the doubt drudger feigns any involvement in this sabotage! Hindsight is always 20/20.

If we sincerely seek to be healed, evil must be addressed.

The solution to this scenario is prayer and obedience. Pray into everything and never stop doing so. By everything, I mean *everything!*

No area should be off limits to God. There should be no "keep out" signs on the closets and cupboards of your life. If there are, deal with them now!

Do everything with prayer as the Word tells us. The minute we become convinced to skirt around a thing that we know to be the express will of God, is the moment we know the saboteur is in that. He strives to keep us off-center about it. He wants to sabotage every dream. Be vigilant and pray him out of your spiritual house in order that the dream can be accomplished for God's glory and for the joy set before us.

God delights in the joy He knows will come to us when something He's given to us gets done right! When a project of any kind, given by God to you, is accomplished with the right intention, in the right manner, and for the right purpose, stick with it to the very end. Do not take shortcuts with God. God is not a corner-cutter!

The doubt drudger's method of operation is to suggest there is a ghost in the machine. No, there is not. Those are his seeds of doubt. Again, pray into every step of your dream, and don't proceed with it until you have done that. Pray over layer upon blessed layer, knowing you have sown God into the fabric of that dream from top to bottom! Do not be persuaded otherwise on this matter of prayer. Be tenacious in it!

Don't let anything about this picture discourage you. Spending time in prayer will only cause you to want to finish what you are doing, with every fiber of your being and just as God called you to do it! As we pray, He strengthens and guides us on our way.

Watch Your Mouth!

The enemy also tries to talk people out of their inheritance (telling them not to enter Canaan), insisting that they need to turn around. He tells them that God is not with them or in the thing they were working on. Don't ever discourage another unless you have prayed about it yourself and the Holy Spirit has given you leeway to say something. Even then, proceed with humble caution in the "how" of your verbal or written delivery system. Many people have inadvertently acted as dream-killers in this way. Dreams are given by God. Dreams are accomplished through God in prayer and with a lot of hard work. Do not stomp on another's dream from God. Watch your mouth and actions, and don't let the enemy use your mouth to sow his evil seeds of doubt into another's garden patch!

Listen to God-given revelation first and foremost. The doubt drudger uses "woe" or "whoa" all the time. We have God's direction, but the devil says, "Woe. That's not as good as it looks. Nope, there's something wrong with this. God's cheating you out of the power you ought to have, you know, to be as He is!" Same old tune, isn't it?

Or just as before, we have God's direction, and the doubter says, "Whoa!" As in, "Let's stop any progress here!" He does this because he sees that you're doing well, and he wants to press a stick into the spokes of your dreams from God. Neither woe nor whoa are from God. Let's look at the Genesis story again: The saboteur got at, or got to, God's own creation through the words of his and her mouth. All was lost in that moment: intimacy, joy, purity, power, relationship, oneness, unity, life, peace, and so much more.

The doubter comes to stop or slow down God's forward momentum through people. How? Often by giving them another vision in its place. The one God called Adam's "helpmate" or "helper" (created out of Adam's own body) was the devil's tool! The devil used Eve (Adam's helpmate) to trip him (Adam) up. This can happen the other way around too.

In the Bible, Abigail showed great wisdom and generosity and stopped David from making a grave mistake. In the middle of David's haste to assuage his righteous anger, which had swiftly flamed from blush to bloom, Abigail spoke words of peace and calm, exhorting David not to be dissuaded from God's plan and path! This is what she said:

> Pardon your servant, my lord, and let me speak to you; hear what your servant has to say. Please pay no attention, my lord, to that wicked man Nabal. He is just like his name— his name means Fool, and folly goes with him. And as for me, your servant, I did not see the men my lord sent. And now, my lord, as surely as the LORD your God lives and as you live, since the LORD has kept you from bloodshed and from avenging yourself with your own hands, may your enemies and all who are intent on harming my lord be like Nabal. (1 Samuel 25:24-26 NIV)

When we know the enemy's ways, we can refuse to act as his pawn! We can refuse his fingers of manipulation in our life prayerfully. We can refuse to allow him to use our mouth unpleasantly, or to cloud our thoughts or darken our heart. We can say no to his vile whispers or his vicious prodding to hurry our actions. We do not have to agree with his plans and allow our feet to run toward evil in a situation; we can hand God the car keys instead!

We can set our feet in a different direction. Even though this deception is thoroughly nasty, it is up to us to stop it and call him out in Jesus's name. As believers, we do this by Jesus's authority. Let's assess our life and repent if repentance is needed. Do not put this off for another day. If we're going to root out the putrid, we've got to get down and dirty. We must get serious!

If the dreams God has given you are to be accomplished—the ones that will fill your heart with satisfaction and joy—you must battle against anything that would keep you from that goal. Take stock right now of the dreams the Lord has given you.

Chapter 4

Belief Stealer

According to God's Word, the serpent can be none other than the evil one himself. He's called "the serpent" or "that old serpent" in the Word of God (Revelation 12:9), as well as other names we'll examine. Unbelief is his first line of attack. If he can get you to that point, he can move you to do *anything*.

Isaiah 59 outlines the power of sin, and I encourage you to read that chapter in its entirety. It illuminates the far-reaching consequences of sin in people but includes God's answer as well. It says that when God saw no help for man, it displeased Him. It also traces how the devil can enter through our own sin. The more we refuse to get a grip on sin and toss it out like the rubbish it is, the more it begins to lay waste to our belief in—and adherence to—God. We lose our footing, and our hope falters. Our sin begins to erode our belief in God as the devil worms his way in, trying to get us to give up on life and faith.

We must not be deceived and give up our hope. The belief stealer will attempt to convince us with thoughts like, You'll never overcome this. You'll always be like this. You are beyond help. You might as well cash in your chips and be done with it already! As the father of lies, he attacks our beliefs, leading us into a morass of devilish, soul-wrenching lies about ourselves. They'll come from multiple sources: a neighbor, a parent, a teacher, words we were told in our youth, words we read, or even through someone involved in the occult that is intentionally cursing us (that does happen). The point is that the enemy's messaging is all around us, trying to bury us alive in his "slough of despond," as John Bunyan called it in The Pilgrim's Progress:

> This miry slough is such a place as cannot be mended; it is the descent whither the scum and filth that attends conviction for sin doth continually run, and therefore is it called the Slough of Despond: for still as the sinner is awakened about his lost condition, there ariseth in his soul many fears, and doubts, and discouraging apprehensions, which all of them get together, and settle in this place; and this is the reason of the badness of this ground.

This is the power of sin. Jesus died to break its hold over mankind, opening a way of freedom for His followers. We need to be washed by Him daily. Otherwise, unresolved sin can make inroads for satan.

This state of hopelessness can produce further trauma and even traumatize someone else in the process. This cycle continues, perpetuating whatever sin is at the root of it all. To triumph over it, we must unearth and destroy it with God's help, as He always intended. We must deal with these problems seriously, and cry out to God, or ask a friend or pastor to intercede for us. Do not let the saboteur lock you into one of his escape rooms—hemmed in with no windows, no doors, no possible exit, overwrought and tormented by lies. His riddling makes your mind tired. Wearing people down in this manner is one of his most commonly used tactics.

The enemy loves to maneuver us into tight spaces so he can torture us and watch us squirm. His goal is to finally deceive you into acting out the lie he has conceived for you—like a viper's egg hatching in your mind. Cut off his deceptive voices in your life, wherever you find them, by repenting of the sin of unbelief. Enlist God to help you immediately! Why do I call them voices? Because the voice of lust comes with a different siren call than that of depression or suicide or violence, though they all have the same evil source.

No matter what, when you hear any of them, get help. Call someone who truly knows God and pray with them, for starters. Begin to praise God. The devil hates this. Think of everything He has ever done for you—large or small—and go to town thanking God for every piece of it. Don't be stingy with your praise to God. Take your time. Give Him the gift of your time and relationship. Give God your *best* praise! As you do this, God will help you in this fight.

Over time, your praise will mature, but you must start somewhere with your praise life. Play worship music in the space you occupy. The belief stealer will do his best to agitate, regurgitate, wiggle into your thoughts, and remind you of bitter moments or words, trying to get your thoughts recentered on the "unlovely" and take you back into his life-sapping lifestyle. Don't let him. Choose to think differently. Choose to do this:

> Finally, brethren, whatever things are true, whatever things are noble, whatever things are just, whatever things are pure, whatever things are lovely, whatever things are of good report, if there is any virtue and if there is anything praiseworthy—meditate on these things. (Philippians 4:8)

This is not a cutesy idea for religious people; this is a heavenly prescription from the Great Physician Himself. Initially, we often balk at a new routine. It's a change, and we don't want to shift anything, so we won't do it at first. Eventually, though, it catches up with us in some way, and we begin to see why it might be a good idea to make the change and adjust. Slowly, we transition and grow. It's the same with our spiritual health. We must follow His direction and take Jesus's Word as the loving prescription it is. As we walk in discipline with the Holy Spirit as Guide and Helper, He will help us remove all the bad habits that load us down in sin and unbelief.

Our thoughts can catapult us into a world of hurt. We need to stand against this and deny the devil his due. Refuse the enemy his payment.

He's done nothing for us. Instead, choose to render to God His part, which is the glory due His name because He has done everything for us!

God will be faithful to show us our sins, granting us the gift of repentance, so sin cannot overcome us. God pinpoints and dismantles areas of unbelief and teaches us how to keep Him front and center. On this firm footing, it's time to clean house.

Ask God to reveal any areas in your life in which the enemy has gained a foothold. Take a spiritual inventory of yourself, inside and out. Ask the Holy Spirit if there is anything in your home, physically or spiritually, that needs to be thrown out. In the physical, cleanse your living space of objects that remind you of past sin (drug or sexual paraphernalia, occult items, art, and so on).

The elevation of self is the gospel of our culture, and it's being preached loud and clear.

You may even need to cut ties with any bad influencers in your life, possibly those you have called friends who are still pulling you further into the abyss of unbelief. Anyone who asks you to take them to a bar or other harmful place, when they know you are mentally or emotionally suffering, is not your friend. They are intent in their practice of sin, and they don't care if you are going against your convictions. Pay attention to what the saboteur is up to in your life. Be careful! Take this seriously.

In the New Testament, "leaven" or "yeast" represents this process.[7] Why? Yeast or leaven in bread makes it rise. This "rising" is a picture of choosing belief in self over belief in God's desire and purpose for your life. The elevation of self is the gospel of our culture, and it's being preached loud and clear. We want to elevate God so that He might lift us up in due time (when you are ready and not before). Have you ever taken bread out of the oven before it was ready? God is the baker! When

---

7. See 1 Corinthians 5:7; Galatians 5:9.

you don't routinely deal with leaven (or the pride of life), it rises and multiplies itself into greater amounts of unbelief, pride, egoism, and the list goes on. As we've just learned, we are not progressing but regressing when we take the broad path of self, the culture around us, and the way of the saboteur, over the life we have in Christ. That life is a far better choice.

Belief is a matter of trust, isn't it? Just like doubt, the seed of unbelief develops bad fruit. Dig out unbelief, roots and all! If you genuinely don't know where a belief-stealing doubt came into your life, ask the Holy Spirit to show you, and then deal with it in prayer. Ask for forgiveness for fostering it. The devil can only make suggestions, but choosing to disbelieve is an act of your will. You can stop it. Remember, the saboteur is an instigator, a pot-stirrer trying to bring about every kind of vice through any enticement. God will never lead you to such a place. But understand this: What you choose to think about matters. You will act according to the way you think. You will act in accordance with the thoughts you believe.

Your mind is a theater, and you are responsible for the movies you show in it. Do not let the saboteur play his movies in this sacred space that you already apportioned to God when you got saved. If you have asked Jesus into your life as the Savior of your soul, then you do not belong to the devil.

If you do not know Jesus, *take care of that* right now. Ask Jesus into your life and repent of your sin. Know that Jesus lived, died, and rose again from the dead *for you!* He walked in obedience as the Son of God *for you.* He came down in the fragility of human flesh and died a horrific death *for you.* Believe in Him today. Confess your sin to Him and be specific. If you have never before prayed to receive Jesus as your Savior and Lord, I invite you to pray this prayer now:

Lord Jesus, I believe in You and in Your great love. Thank You for dying on the cross so I may be forgiven of my sins and live eternally with You beginning right now. I repent for all of my sins, and I turn away from them now. I receive Your forgiveness and Your grace to go forward in this life as a new creation. I love You.

If you just prayed that prayer, all of heaven is rejoicing, and I rejoice with you as well. Now you can walk in newness of life with Him and begin to enjoy a life of peace, rather than one in direct opposition to Him. Find fellowship with other Bible-believing, Jesus-loving saints. Tell them about your new confession of faith, and start moving with intention in the ways of God. Foil the enemy, but don't let him fool you!

Jesus wants us to take Him up on His offers to help us, and He expects us to listen to His good counsel. In fact, one of the names of God is Wonderful Counselor (Isaiah 9:6). Do you need a counselor? Jesus is the best One ever!

Whether you confessed your belief in Jesus for the first time, or you are coming to Him for the fiftieth time, He greets you with open arms. Consider any areas of unbelief that the Holy Spirit has pointed out to you and pray over them now. Ask Him daily to highlight any area in which you need His help. He is faithful to guide us into all truth.

Chapter 5

Diametric Deceiver

Beloved, do not believe every spirit, but test the spirits, whether they are of God; because many false prophets have gone out into the world. By this you know the Spirit of God: Every spirit that confesses that Jesus Christ has come in the flesh is of God, and every spirit that does not confess that Jesus Christ has come in the flesh is not of God. And this is the spirit of the Antichrist, which you have heard was coming, and is now already in the world. You are of God, little children, and have overcome them, because He who is in you is greater than he who is in the world. They are of the world. Therefore they speak as of the world, and the world hears them. We are of God. He who knows God hears us; he who is not of God does not hear us. By this we know the spirit of truth and the spirit of error. (1 John 4:1-6)

False prophets are the enemy's deceivers. At the writing of this book, this topic has come to the forefront in the mind of many. We're seeing a heightened panic and a dogged determination to root out the rot! While that's not a bad idea, it falls short when we start "shooting our own" in that righteous-minded hunt.

The genuine church of Jesus followers has been remiss in recognizing modern-day pundits and influencers as false prophets. We look only in the church, but since we only look there, we unwittingly fall into the saboteur's trap, missing the everyday obvious false prophets operating outside of the church.

In God's Word, His prophets had various professions. Many of them were farmers, herdsmen, shepherds, sons of priests, or servants to the king, like politicians and government workers. Some held other occupations, but they were each called specifically by God to speak to their generation.

The saboteur has always worked seamlessly with governments and secular agencies of any kind to elevate his own "mouthpieces" or "spokespersons" into the positions where he wants them. He juggles many, including entertainers, sports figures, successful businesspeople, musicians, artists, authors, and teachers. Just as God anoints His prophets to prophesy truth, the devil grants a counter-anointing, a satanic one, to his human agents through demonic power.

While it is true that false prophets operate inside and outside of the church, and that's where the yellow caution tape needs to be applied first, we mustn't sweep past the fact that we've made this mistake. We've relegated the existence of false prophets to those on the periphery of the church (in para-church ministries) or inside of the church proper. Nowhere else.

We are surrounded by actual (and some would-be) false prophets, many in influential positions, such as talk show hosts, podcasters, inspirational speakers, pastors, philosophers, bishops, musicians, athletes, celebrities, and even some worship artists. Some false prophets occupy pulpits, and some do not; either way, they are the false prophets of this hour. This generation, more than any before it, is hyper-focused on the demise of God's people. Why? The demonic realm can sense the preparation for the final harvest of souls into God's kingdom, and the enemy is fixed on aborting it. The saboteur is fixated on abortion in every sense of the word.

To help you grasp this concept, picture a dirty coach preparing his team by teaching them to employ the ugliest of underhanded tactics you can imagine to "win" the game. Got the picture? Now, darken that lens to the inkiest of blackest-black, and you might get a slight glimpse of what the saboteur is capable of effecting through his false prophets. He uses them to mock, tear down, eradicate, and dismember God's true church and those considering following Jesus. The saboteur's 24/7 game-face can be summed up in three words: steal, kill, and destroy. This is how Jesus described him (John 10:10). The saboteur's nature stays the same all the time. Without fail, he will be executing robbery, plotting murder, and seeking destruction wherever you find him or his compatriots.

Some false prophets of this hour are aware of what they are doing, but others are not enlightened as to their role. Nevertheless, in God's estimation, that is what they are. You can learn to spot an antichrist spirit (a false prophet) by rereading 1 John 4:1-6.

Understand that they have gone out into the world, and the world hears them. Why does the world listen to them? Because they are influencers, but in the wrong direction, while true prophets are influencers in the right direction. Not every non-believer is a false prophet. However, any influencer of great masses of people who is pointing others in the wrong direction is acting like a false prophet. People are listening and going the wrong way. As Westerners, we struggle with the idea of the demonic realm, and because of that, we often do not see the dangers in the world clearly.

However, every demonic power is well aware of the struggle and has bent their will to use all influencers through whom they can operate to sway great numbers of people away from God. Satan knows his time is short. The demons and the spiritual hosts of wickedness in the heavenly places know this too. This does not mean that everyone who does not influence for God is a false prophet, but noting how someone in any field sways those who are listening to them is a good gauge of their true nature. This is tricky with the unwitting, but a false prophet will steer people away from God and not toward Him.

For years, the church has deemed "those prosperity gospel people" or "those name-it-and-claim-it teachers" or even the "tongue-talking folk" as false prophets. This is an extremely small-minded perspective. Meanwhile, we have ignored the forces that have manipulated the masses in dark, antichrist directions on every layer of society at large, as well as those inside the church.

The false prophet arena is full of mainstream media talking heads, top musicians and authors, sports figures, comedians, politicians, corporate tycoons, scientists, and more. They are the most read and most listened to people on the face of this earth. When we change our perspective on what a false prophet is, and stop shooting our brethren, we will immediately be more effective in our prayer life and spiritual growth. This is the height of sabotage, and the devil has a huge belly laugh whenever he sees the church killing each other off. It creates quite a sensation among his fallen angel sympathizers.

Believers don't shoot each other because of their differences. The church is made up of many who adore and worship God but do not look like one another or act like one another. We are a beautiful bouquet of diversity. This does not mean we have license to throw out portions of God's Word because they are inconvenient to our lifestyle in some way, so there is still a just and righteous checks and balances system in God's Word that we must follow. We should share our core beliefs with one another to see if they line up with the Word of God, but after that, God is the Judge of us all. We need to step back. The saboteur's primary mission is to kill off believers, and it is God's position to act as Judge, not ours.

> For the idols speak delusion; the diviners envision lies, and tell false dreams; they comfort in vain. Therefore the people wend their way like sheep; they are in trouble because there is no shepherd. (Zechariah 10:2)

Southern California has a weather condition that shows up from time to time called an inversion layer. This happens when air temperature increases as it gets higher above the ground. The condition runs counter to the normal decrease in temperature with height. That's how this inversion occurs.

An *inversion* is a reversal of the normal order of things. This cap, a meteorological phenomenon, is where you find this haze-like, trapped layer of weather. To the naked eye, it manifests as a layer of air that is fog-like but not as dense. Sometimes it can sit in valleys or cling to the lower skirt of the California coastal range near where I've lived most of my life. Because of it, we could have a crystalline California day or a far blurrier view, at least until air temperatures normalize.

Anytime our perception is skewed by a condition that obscures our vision, we are not seeing things as they really are. Decisions are made, beliefs held, and paths pursued in ignorance of reality. This is truly alarming.

Anytime our perception is skewed by a condition that obscures our vision, we are not seeing things as they really are.

God identifies Himself as Light (the true Light). He is also the Way. That means His very essence places a high value on clarity, illumination, and right direction. God cannot act against His nature, nor can He deceive.

Paul taught that he could be identified by the way he presented himself, as one who had "the truth of Christ in me" (2 Corinthians 11:10). He warns too that there are false apostles—deceitful workers transforming themselves into apostles of Christ. Wanting the church to be prepared to discern correctly, he said something shocking—or is it? Paul wrote this:

> Satan himself transforms himself into an angel of light. Therefore it is no great thing if his ministers also transform themselves into ministers of righteousness, whose end will be according to their works. (2 Corinthians 11:14-15)

We can know whether or not we are in the truth by looking at the fruit in our life. Through prayer and discernment given by the Spirit of Truth, God faithfully develops His fruit in our heart and life.

My pastor, Kevin Lewis, puts it this way: "Even though we don't see the roots below ground, we know people by the fruit of their lives that we see above the ground. We can tell if it's an orange, a lemon, or a pomegranate tree by the fruit."

In the same way, spiritually speaking, what's growing in your root system is displayed above-ground in how you "operate" or "manage" your life. Are you a liar, a gossip, an adulterer, a cheater, or any of the others outlined in Galatians 5:16-26? The "fruit" just mentioned is only a few of the types of seeds the saboteur loves to plant in your life garden. They will lead you to an end that separates you eternally from God, so this is no joke. If you need God's help with bad fruit in your heart, ask Him for help.

The saboteur is a diametric deceiver. The word *diametric* highlights just how serious he is about weaving his deception into your root system. He wants the good purposes God has for you to be aborted—never to see the light of day or come to fruition.

How do we take spiritual weedkiller to the oppositional forces that feed on the shackles of deception in our life? Tackle them head-on: Pray. Confess and repent of known sin. Steep yourself in God's Word, and use it to retrain your whole being: heart, mind, body, and soul. Invite the Holy Spirit to help you walk in the opposite direction. He will help you change your mind and heart patterns, turning back all the pieces that brought you into this bleak spiritual wilderness in the first place. He'll help you walk in the opposite direction. Note that He'll actually help you walk, not just give you the option. It's not like a gym membership. I have it, but I never go, so my body looks the same and is growing worse by the day. No, Jesus actively helps us walk.

It might be helpful to invite an accountability partner into the new habitual patterns you are electing to follow. A friend is a great help so we don't fall off the wagon. If it took a while to form the patterns—and it usually does—be patient with yourself as you establish new ones. You may fall, but God will not drop you. He loves you and is for you! He understands the intricacies of the saboteur's deceptive ways and how they are in direct opposition to His truth.

> For there is nothing hidden which will not be revealed, nor has anything been kept secret but that it should come to light. (Mark 4:22)

> For many deceivers have gone out into the world who do not confess Jesus Christ as coming in the flesh. This is a deceiver and an antichrist. (2 John 1:7)

Deceptive people are everywhere, and they are good at the bad they do. Some of them are so good at it that they consider it an art. They pride themselves for cheating others out of what was rightfully theirs; they do this through lies. And the Bible says this state will only grow darker.

But we are not to stay home and pull the drapes! God wants us to be aware of the darkness, but He especially wants us "out there" bringing light into it, so that souls who are being duped by the enemy can be brought out of the kingdom of darkness and into His blessed kingdom of light! To do this, we must walk wisely.

Examine what people say and pay attention to their fruit. Listen well, talk to the Lord when you have a question, listen to the Holy Spirit within you, and let Him guide you. This seems so simple, but for many who are naïve, it is not.

There are many with evil intentions who follow in the art of deception like their father, the saboteur. We often think we can spot a deceiver easily, but that's not usually the case. In fact, this is why God gave us His Holy Spirit. We need the Spirit of Truth to help us because the enemy is not easy to spot.

Make decisions based on the true data given you by the Holy Spirit rather than what your eyes tell you. Some "deep fakes" are just that—*fake!* Christ followers do not have to deal in best guesses or their own estimates, but on the true data given by a blessed Savior who lives in you.

When you meet, understand, and expose the saboteur in his deceptions, you have come face to face with one of his primary attributes. God's main attributes are love and truth, but the deceiver is nothing like God.

Many say that the devil's premier sin is pride, and it works together with murder and robbery as he seeks to deceive. An epic thief, he uses deception to take what is not his and destroy all he can.

The saboteur cannot tell the truth of who he is, nor does he have the inclination to do so. Please read that last statement again.

> **The saboteur cannot tell the truth of who he is, nor does he have the inclination to do so.**

Does this sound like someone you'd want to be joined with? An adulterous relationship with the diametric deceiver will always be ruinous. Any agreement made with him is adulterous because we are made in God's image and belong with God. Many are not aware of this fact, but the devil surely is.

He knows his mission and that his time to complete it is short. Again, his mission in our life is to marry us into all his deadly debauchery and evil, and then divorce us, destroying us in the process. His plan is to take people down the aisle of life, introducing them to anything that will lead them away from God, with malice in his non-existent heart. *Love* is a word the devil does not know. It is the antithesis of who and what he is in his essence. Take a moment and form a picture in your mind of this evil being who is intent on the destruction of mankind, simply because of his hatred for our Father.

Everyone has heard this saying: "My mama told me to stay away from boys like you!" Every girl in my age group not only heard this but knew what it meant. I'm sure there are many similar phrases used to convey unacceptable choices. For a guy, these were those you could not "bring home to Mama." They were not an acceptable choice for a young person to marry.

Some people think they can toy with a so-called "bad boy" or a "Delilah." Go to Judges 16 for a closer look. Delilah was a prostitute who was used to ensnare a judge. Samson was miraculously born and appointed by God. He was supposed to be God's gracious gift—His answer sent to relieve Israel of the vicious stranglehold that another nation had placed upon them.

Their cyclical rebellions against God had placed them in this position in the first place, but God heard their cries in their trouble and sent Samson to deliver them! However, even though Samson was a judge and divinely sent, he dabbled with Delilah because he thought he could handle it. He treated God's firm *no* with disdain. The book of Proverbs appeals repeatedly to both sons and daughters to watch out for those with a seductive spirit. It is not just a metaphor. Seductive spirits reside in men and women and are acutely skilled at their trade!

Anyone filled with a seductive spirit will lead you down to the pit. Misery does love company. We need to listen to the things we say. Out of our heart our mouth speaks, so we need to check ourselves. Do you find yourself talking about someone you are attracted to in ways that go over the lines? Or it could be something else entirely—some sparkly object that has caught your eye? In either case, are you making excuses and allowances for those feelings, giving them airtime and room in your heart?

Meanwhile, the voice of wisdom is disregarded. You know this desire is wrong and could even be disastrous for you, but *you think you can handle it* for a while, maybe a month, or just one weekend of fun. Yeah, Samson thought so too. If you are there, the deceiver has laid a plan to sabotage your life. Once you've done it one time, you are wide open to creating a habit. Pull up the stakes and ask Jesus for His help! Wait. God's words for us are well expressed in Proverbs 5:

> For the lips of the adulterous woman drip honey,
> and her speech is smoother than oil;
> but in the end she is bitter as gall,
> sharp as a double-edged sword.
> Her feet go down to death;

> her steps lead straight to the grave.
> She gives no thought to the way of life;
> her paths wander aimlessly, but she does not know it.
>
> Now then, my sons, listen to me;
> do not turn aside from what I say.
> Keep to a path far from her,
> do not go near the door of her house,
> lest you lose your honor to others
> and your dignity to one who is cruel.
> Proverbs 5:3-9 (NIV)

Another method of deception is through pride. The diametric deceiver sells both young men and young women on the idea that they are unlike any previous generation, so they discount the wisdom of those who have gone before them. Without the sense that years and experience bring, they make choices that have longstanding repercussions for their life. God offers wisdom and prudence to keep them safe!

> My son, if sinful men entice you,
> do not give in to them.
> If they say, "Come along with us;
> let's lie in wait for innocent blood,
> let's ambush some harmless soul;
> let's swallow them alive, like the grave,
> and whole, like those who go down to the pit;
> we will get all sorts of valuable things
> and fill our houses with plunder;
> cast lots with us;
> we will all share the loot"—
> my son, do not go along with them,
> do not set foot on their paths;
> for their feet rush into evil,
> they are swift to shed blood.
> Proverbs 1:10-16 (NIV)

The devil will place you on the altar of destruction; in fact, he already sees you there. That altar is not a marital altar; it is the altar of your sacrifice. You are a sacrifice the devil is fully willing to make if he can get you to listen to him. However, your Maker is not willing to give you up so easily, and He did something about it! His deliverance is readily available right now. Out of His pure love for us, He reaches to deliver us, especially the young who lack wisdom.

My mother's heart aches for the millions of children led to destruction, generation after generation. The saboteur has been at his game for a very long time, and he knows that we, without God's help, will fail in our attempts to "be good." Only God is good, to be sure, but He has given us the tools we need to combat the deceiving forces around us. As we pay attention to God's warnings in our life, He will lead us to dismiss the saboteur in the powerful name of Jesus! Jesus's name, His blood, and His Word are more than enough to combat the enemy—no matter what anyone has told you to the contrary.

Chapter 6

Blustering Blasphemer

Blasphemy is a specific sin, but the spirit of mockery and scoffing (both real demonic spirits) can quickly lead to blasphemy. If these particular spirits go unchecked in their resistance to the works of God, they will lead you right into blasphemy, unimpeded. The saboteur puts ideas that mock God into our mind as often as possible. If they solidify in our heart and come out of our mouth, we have made our enemy happy. Why? Because we are part of God's creation—with the image of Christ stamped on us and the breath of life from Him in us. The saboteur deems any perverse turning on God from us as his crowning achievement, his utmost accomplishment. The devil knows we belong to God, and he loves it whenever we "join the other side."

> I watched then because of the sound of the pompous words which the horn was speaking; I watched till the beast was slain, and its body destroyed and given to the burning flame. As for the rest of the beasts, they had their dominion taken away, yet their lives were prolonged for a season and a time. (Daniel 7:11-12)

What is a blusterer? Like in the scripture verse above, he speaks pompous words. You may have met a person like this, but how does the saboteur manifest this? He is loud, aggressive, indignant, arrogant, manipulative, self-absorbed and selfish, insistent, controlling, insensitive in every way, and full of threats. However, he will very often *not* carry through with his threats.

We see evidence for this in the book of Nehemiah. The devil is a liar. The demonic blusterers in Nehemiah were Sanballat, Tobiah, and Geshem. As Nehemiah rebuilt the wall of Jerusalem, they opposed him in every way they could. I encourage you to read the book of Nehemiah to see how he overcame these men who were sent by the enemy to stand against him.

We see this again in 2 Kings 19, where he shows up as Sennacherib's Rabshakeh, his chief officer, who was sent to loudly stir up fear in the people of God. All of these men were sent to thwart the work of God. They openly mocked God's work and claimed He would not save His people.

It still looks much the same in today's world. Mockers and scoffers are evidence of the satanic work around us. If the mocking and scoffing doesn't work, they move to threats, manipulation, and eventually, serious attempts on our life. Why does this blaspheming blusterer do this to us?

He simply wants to stop us from making any God-driven progress. He is trying to get us to stop from moving forward with God's plan. If he can frighten us away from our post by believing his lies and arrogant claims, he has succeeded in keeping us from walking in obedience to God's directives. Let's not be pushovers in the kingdom. Stand! We must be immoveable!

> If you do not stand firm in your faith, you will not stand
> at all. (Isaiah 7:9b NIV)

By standing and resisting him, we stand with our Redeemer. We stand just as our Savior surely stood for us—against all odds. Though innocent of all crimes, Jesus took our punishment on Himself in obedience to His Father's will. In the same way, we must stand and not succumb to the enemy's lies and boisterous outbursts of manipulative trash talk. Have you ever seen a staged fight for PR purposes? The opposing fighters will trash talk each other, calling out their weaknesses, using expletives, and speaking boastfully about themselves and how they will defeat one another. Our enemy does the same. A king in 2 Chronicles 32 had to deal with just such a precarious situation. The story goes like this:

> This is what Sennacherib king of Assyria says: On what are you basing your confidence, that you remain in Jerusalem under siege? When Hezekiah says, "The LORD our God will save us from the hand of the king of Assyria," he is misleading you, to let you die of hunger and thirst. Did not Hezekiah himself remove this god's high places and altars, saying to Judah and Jerusalem, "You must worship before one altar and burn sacrifices on it"?
>
> Do you not know what I and my predecessors have done to all the peoples of the other lands? Were the gods of those nations ever able to deliver their land from my hand? Who of all the gods of these nations that my predecessors destroyed has been able to save his people from me? How then can your god deliver you from my hand? Now do not let Hezekiah deceive you and mislead you like this. Do not believe him, for no god of any nation or kingdom has been able to deliver his people from my hand or the hand of my predecessors. How much less will your god deliver you from my hand! (2 Chronicles 32:10-15 NIV)

In the end, this awful scenario ended well. The reason it did was because King Hezekiah made an excellent choice in that moment. He did not lean on his own understanding. Instead, Hezekiah sought God in his hour of trial. He took the threats of the saboteur and laid them out before God. And God had the final word.

When we find ourselves between a rock and a hard place, with no exit in sight, we must remember that God is with us. The enemy gets pleasure by our belief that we're hemmed in and in one of his escape rooms—that we're truly stuck with no way out. If you are there right now, remind yourself that the devil is a liar and a deceiver, and he is an expert at it. The apostle Paul wrote this to the early church when they were dealing with huge personal difficulties:

> Whatever happens, conduct yourselves in a manner worthy of the gospel of Christ. Then, whether I come and see you or only hear about you in my absence, I will know that you stand firm in the one Spirit, striving together as one for the faith of the gospel without being frightened in any way by those who oppose you. This is a sign to them that they will be destroyed, but that you will be saved—and that by God. For it has been granted to you on behalf of Christ not only to believe in him, but also to suffer for him, since you are going through the same struggle you saw I had, and now hear that I still have. (Philippians 1:27-30 NIV)

God is always with us. He is *in* us. We may suffer, but we are never alone in it. In fact, God uses suffering to bring us even closer to His heart than we were before. That is another aspect of our life that the enemy does not understand. He thinks that we, like him, will turn on God.

Through blasphemy, he tries to steal that which is uniquely God's work and God's design.

Now let's look at the other title he possesses: the blasphemer. Through blasphemy, he tries to steal that which is uniquely God's work and God's design. Remember, the title of God is his dearest wish for himself. Historically, many of the pharaohs of Egypt had their own names carved into various projects, not giving credit to the actual builder. This is a perfect, real-world example of what the enemy of our soul does too. When the Bible says he steals, it isn't a metaphor. He steals every good thing of ours that he can get his grubby hands on. He has a thief mentality!

It is important that we understand his plan because it is our life that he attempts to seize. The building blocks (all of us) were made by God. When the blasphemer uses people to put together a twisted and corrupted version of God's intent, he is claiming that he is the maker and creator of it all. He wants the glory for this thing he cobbled together. Jesus expects us to cry out like the child in *The Emperor's New Clothes*: "Why is the emperor naked? He's not wearing any clothes at all!" We don't want to be the hoodwinked king in that story, so we must stay in the Word and be sure that our life is built on a strong foundation in Christ. None of us wants to be waylaid in this matter.

There is no wiggle room on this one. Everyone must study to show himself or herself approved (2 Timothy 2:15 KJV). It does not take a degree or special ability to understand the Bible. As we invite the Holy Spirit into our Bible study sessions, He will lead us into all truth and guide us in the way we should go, just as He promises. God wants to see a committed and true heart, not one that ignores His ways.

God looks for a passionate love for Him and His Word in all of us. We need both to remain strong. Without a balance, we will end up with lots of knowledge or an overemphasis on works, but not the spiritually healthy life God wants for us. God grows us by the power of His Holy Spirit without striving in fleshly efforts and strain. If we rely on those, we will fail. All of us fail when we strive in our own strength. Not owning this fact is a sign of immaturity.

The way of success requires a daily leaning on Christ—learning to invite Him to help you *every* time, not just sometimes. That is part of our problem. Sometimes we don't want God looking over our shoulder. When we recognize that kind of thinking, we know we just found a "pocket" in our faith that needs immediate attention. It is these sin pockets that give the devil a toehold in an effort to make our life unpleasant. If this issue is not tended, it will not go away or mend itself. It will grow, so deal with it rather than ignore it. Jesus wants us to bring these issues straight to Him so He can help us. Avoiding them never makes them go away.

To understand blasphemy better, pay attention to the way Jesus was tempted after fasting for many weeks in Luke 4:1-13. The devil tried to abort Jesus's mission assigned to Him by the heavenly Father *before* He even got started in His teaching ministry. Jesus shows us how we should manage such onslaughts. The saboteur will not treat us with any caution or show us any special leniency because we're a newcomer to our faith. We are, in fact, exactly the kind of untested target he likes to hit *before* we begin to mature in Christ.

God grows us by the power of His Holy Spirit without striving in fleshly efforts and strain.

He's always doing the same old thing; he came after Jesus *before* He got started too. We must remember that our spiritual firepower is far greater than the satanic pride we are dealing with. However, the enemy hopes you do not know that so he can wound you at the start of your walk with Jesus. His goal is to sabotage that relationship. He wants to nip it in the bud. The last thing he wants is to deal with the fruit we will bear from our relationship with our Savior!

He wants to cut us off at the knees! An ugly picture, but an accurate one. Anyone with faith in Jesus Christ must expect to be waylaid by this highwayman behind his mask. That doesn't mean there is a devil under every bush; there isn't. Our concern is in dealing with hostile attacks in our path. In this case, the spiritual discipline every believer needs to practice is humility. In martial arts, like karate and the like, you cannot move up to the next color belt until you have mastered each requirement for it.

Advancement is dependent on understanding, not age. Similarly, our maturity in the Lord does not always follow our age in Jesus (how long we've been saved); instead, it depends on our willingness to bow low in humility and walk in obedience. Let that sink in. It is the polar opposite of the secular world's concept of success.

Jesus will never—and I mean never—use the same methodology as the saboteur. Their ways are nothing alike. Jesus does not trap, waylay, bait and switch, or seek to harm us. The saboteur will do all of that with great vigor! The Lord does not tempt us or willfully trip us up. That is not God's way. This is a key principle about His nature we would do well to hold fast. God is wholly good and will only do good in our life.

He is protective. He might awaken you to danger as any Good Shepherd of the sheep would do (John 10:11-14). He's not about to let one of His dear lambs fall headlong into a canyon without taking any action, so we may feel the touch of His rod or staff to keep us on the way, but Jesus is never abusive. That word will never describe Him. Jesus will never hurt us. He will only guide us away from pitfalls and traps that we do not recognize in our immaturity or ignorance. But He is watching over us for good, not evil.

Do not let anyone—believer or not—tell you that Jesus puts out trip-wires to teach us lessons. It is amazing how many opinions those who know nothing about God's Word have come up with about how God does or does not work. Do not listen to the opinions of others. It's that simple. Would we take lessons on how to fly a plane from someone who hasn't been certified to fly a plane? Nope. So let's not listen to anyone who does not know God. They cannot speak for Him. Opinionated non-believers are interesting, but they are not yet at peace with God, so they are not our best source of spiritual wisdom, as they can only offer earthly wisdom.

God has a voice. God has a way. God has His inerrant written Word. Listen to the Holy Spirit and learn from Him.

Jesus's powerful usage of holy Scripture shines in His exchange with satan in Luke 4. Over and over again, He countered with, "It is written." Jesus modeled this use of His Word to us for a reason. He expects us to emerge victorious and with flying colors using the same method. Take notes from Jesus—our Teacher and Rabbi (John 3:2), and steep yourself in His Word.

We already highlighted how the deceiver was in the garden, but the very first use of blasphemy also occurred in that garden. The serpent tells Eve:

> For God knows that in the day you eat of it your eyes will
> be opened, and you will be like God, knowing good and
> evil. (Genesis 3:5)

Where is the lie in that? Simply this: Eve could never be like God in the sense of a duplicate of Him—not ever! And this goes beyond being a simple lie, as he was telling Eve that God had withheld something from her—something good. He was insinuating that God had purposefully kept something from both of them that would benefit them. What a blasphemous lie! God would never withhold anything He knew was good for His beloved creation. It is deeply foundational to know that it is not in God's nature to do such a thing! Satan knew he was slandering the Holy One's character when he did this.

To grasp the depth of his crime, think about this: satan formed a plan to destroy God's great treasure—a race of people upon whom God had set His love.

Suppose I told you that you could shop in every store in a huge mall, except one small one because it sold poison. That's basically what God told them, but the saboteur highlighted the fact that the fruit looked good and used that as a selling point. To this he added his lie about God's intent, knowing full well that it really was poisonous and deadly.

Every temptation begins with desire and doubt. We want something and feel ill-used over something, so we take actions that hurt us. The devil will try to get us to focus on our small, supposed disappointments so we will diminish any good we see. We doubt God. That is a trap! And it's the same one he used in Eden.

To the first people, that poison did indeed have immediate and deadly consequences, just as God had told Adam.

The enemy questioned God's truthful, faithful nature to His own creation, Eve, while Adam was nearby. After decades of marriage, if someone questioned something about my husband to me, it would be a real fine way to get my hackles up. I know my husband's character. It would feel like a slap in the face. That is genuine faithfulness between a husband and wife; we stand steady for one another, especially if someone targets our character.

Likewise, knowing God is not a one and done kind of thing. It's a relationship, and we need to stay steady in it, just as we do in our marriages.

We can know Him by staying in His Word and interacting with Him in prayer. God is not religious with us; He is relational.

Who wants a relationship with a religious God? I want a relationship with a knowable God, not one who stands aloof, but one who draws near as I draw near to Him (James 4:8).

The devil will try to get us to focus on our small, supposed disappointments so we will diminish any good we see.

Today, this constantly used tactic of the enemy can be seen in advertising, song lyrics, preaching, teaching, prophecy, and propositional phraseology. We disparage God's character and bend it to suggest other meanings. We take things that He alone has uniquely designed and sovereignly planned and attribute them to some other source—possibly the saboteur, worst of all! He will delightedly stand nearby to absorb whatever praise he can siphon off of God's perfect design. He will call it his any day of the week! Those who have had their creative work, art, design, writing, music, or business stolen know the deep pain of someone claiming *your* hard work or creativity as their own.

Watch for the saboteur! He clothes himself in blasphemy. Using it, he tries to confuse or disorient you, and then get you ensnared and tangled in his stinking thinking. Once there, he infiltrates your lifestyle and alters your ways, so they mesh with his thoughts and ways! The apostle Paul wrote this:

> Even though I was once a blasphemer and a persecutor and a violent man, I was shown mercy because I acted in ignorance and unbelief. (1 Timothy 1:13 NIV)

This is never positive, and it is difficult to escape, but the Bible tells us it is never too late. Jesus lives, and His specialty is redemption. If you have found yourself in this situation like the apostle Paul, repent today and receive God's grace and forgiveness.

Again, balance is important to our health. We must not use our freedom in Christ as a license to sin. God calls this *transgression*, and it refers to sin we choose, so it describes walking knowingly *and repeatedly* on the wrong path. Again, you know it, but you lie to yourself. That life-pattern is not from God; it is the saboteur's way. If you stay this kind of course, there is no good ending. Joshua 24:15 says, "Choose for yourselves this day whom you will serve." As Jesus taught, we cannot serve two masters: One will always take the lead and have mastery over the other.

If the saboteur's snaky skill is *cunning* (deceptive coercion), then he is appealing to our flesh (what feels good). This is a useful tactic for him because we are made up of both flesh and spirit. Galatians 5:16-26 outlines this in what we will call the "hall of infamy." Second Timothy 3 describes people led by their flesh.

> For men will be lovers of themselves, lovers of money, boasters, proud, blasphemers, disobedient to parents, unthankful, unholy, unloving, unforgiving, slanderers, without self-control, brutal, despisers of good, traitors, headstrong, haughty, lovers of pleasure rather than lovers of God, having a form of godliness but denying its power. And from such people turn away! (2 Timothy 3:2-5)

Be vigilant against the nuances of the wily saboteur. He is oh so willing to try his schemes out on you. Because he is so subtle, we often do not recognize any of the lies that can slowly creep into our thought life. This is a good time to pause and ask God to show you anything like that in your own life.

Chapter 7

Contemptuous Charlatan

S atan will perpetually attempt to enslave us so God will not be served, worshiped, or obeyed. He wants us to hate God like he does.

If a substantial minority in the West thus deliberately closes its eyes to obvious reality, the explanation may well lie in an unacknowledged desire to live under Stalinism, not in spite of what it is, but because of what it is. Some want to wield the power of a tyrant, a wish from which none of us is free; for others it is the need to submit to a tyrant's rule, and none of us is free from that murky impulse either. After all, if tyranny had never enjoyed the complicity of its victims, the history of our times-and many other times-would have been quite different.

—Jean-Francois Revel[8]

From a position of genuine freedom, this seems a curious statement. On its face, Revel seems to be sharing a political concept, but ultimately, it is spiritual. The saboteur's telltale marks can be found in the root system of every failed government system. He uses governments to reel people into bondage while simultaneously making them believe it is good for them. A

---

8. Jean François Revel, *The Totalitarian Temptation*, trans. David Hapgood (New York: Doubleday, 1977), 25.

thinking person recognizes this as condescending and presumptuous, but his ways are hypnotic.

A father of lies, he offers layers of supposed deeper knowledge through his propaganda in such a way that shackles are no longer necessary. Once refocused by the saboteur, his victims are turned by him to hunt the unshackled spiritually healthy ones who are left. And so it goes.

People are corrupted to believe in an evil system led by those who are ungrounded in the Word and unsubmitted to Holy Spirit authority over them. They are often governed by people who are equally as blind and untethered to God. It is unfortunate but true.

> Let no one deceive you with empty words, for because of these things the wrath of God comes upon the sons of disobedience. Therefore do not be partakers with them. For you were once darkness, but now you are light in the Lord. Walk as children of light (for the fruit of the Spirit is in all goodness, righteousness, and truth), finding out what is acceptable to the Lord. And have no fellowship with the unfruitful works of darkness, but rather expose them. For it is shameful even to speak of those things which are done by them in secret. But all things that are exposed are made manifest by the light, for whatever makes manifest is light. Therefore He says: "Awake, you who sleep, arise from the dead, and Christ will give you light." (Ephesians 5:6-14)

> Adulterers and adulteresses! Do you not know that friendship with the world is enmity with God? Whoever therefore wants to be a friend of the world makes himself an enemy of God. (James 4:4)

Enmity with God is not a goal. The contemptuous charlatan will not only land you there but strap you in and send you to hell. Why mince words? The time is too short to play games.

God's heart toward us is redemption through salvation in Jesus Christ all the time.

> So must the Son of Man be lifted up [referencing Jesus's crucifixion], that whoever believes in Him should not perish but have eternal life. For God so loved the world that He gave His only begotten Son, that whoever believes in Him should not perish but have everlasting life. For God did not send His Son into the world to condemn the world, but that the world through Him might be saved. (John 3:14b-17)

> Even so it is not the will of your Father who is in heaven that one of these little ones should perish. (Matthew 18:14)

The prophet Jonah preached to a grossly violent civilization. He said, "Yet forty days, and Nineveh shall be overthrown!" (Jonah 3:4)

The king heard it and repented immediately, calling his people to adhere to the call:

> But let man and beast be covered with sackcloth, and cry mightily to God; yes, let every one turn from his evil way and from the violence that is in his hands. Who can tell if God will turn and relent, and turn away from His fierce anger, so that we may not perish? (Jonah 3:8-9)

Then God saw:

> Then God saw their works, that they turned from their evil way; and God relented from the disaster that He had said He would bring upon them, and He did not do it. (Jonah 3:10)

Do you think for one second the saboteur saw this coming? Do you think he thought he'd lose this city? No, he thought it was all trussed up like a dead fly for the spider's dinner. But God, in His mercy, clothed in salvation, gave them repentance. In the same way, He looks to redeem us from the fowler's snare!

Those also who seek my life lay snares for me; those who seek my hurt speak of destruction, and plan deception all the day long. (Psalm 38:12)

Surely He shall deliver you from the snare of the fowler and from the perilous pestilence. (Psalm 91:3)

Our soul has escaped as a bird from the snare of the fowlers; the snare is broken, and we have escaped. (Psalm 124:7)

When my spirit was overwhelmed within me, then You knew my path. In the way in which I walk they have secretly set a snare for me. (Psalm 142:3)

Moreover he must have a good testimony among those who are outside, lest he fall into reproach and the snare of the devil. (1 Timothy 3:7)

But those who desire to be rich fall into temptation and a snare, and into many foolish and harmful lusts which drown men in destruction and perdition. (1 Timothy 6:9)

That they may come to their senses and escape the snare of the devil, having been taken captive by him to do his will. (2 Timothy 2:26)

But take heed to yourselves, lest your hearts be weighed down with carousing, drunkenness, and cares of this life, and that Day come on you unexpectedly. For it will come as a snare on all those who dwell on the face of the whole earth. Watch therefore, and pray always that you may be counted worthy to escape all these things that will come to pass, and to stand before the Son of Man. (Luke 21:34-36)

The Contemptuous Charlatan wants to ensnare your life. Through prayer and repentance, see to it that he doesn't get the chance!

Chapter 8

Duplicitous Debonair Debutant

No servant can serve two masters; for either he will hate the one and love the other, or else he will be loyal to the one and despise the other. You cannot serve God and mammon. (Luke 16:13)

Give me a new word I haven't heard before, and I am like a pig in mud (I just made you laugh)! It's a nerdy habit, but it cannot be helped. So if you ever meet me in person, teach me a new word, and we will be instant friends (I hope)! The Holy Spirit (and my dearest friends) know that I simply adore words, and I always will.

So I was not surprised when He spoke to me in the shower about this chapter, and said, "He's also the duplicitous debonair debutant." This chapter could just as easily be called, "Let's talk about *mixture.*"

My husband and I have been in ministry our entire married life. We've been involved with so many types of outreach that I have no doubt forgotten some of them. It's okay though; it all heads directly up to Jesus as a fragrant offering. I have been saved by the grace of God and through the blood of the slain Lamb. I am marked by the Holy Spirit until the blessed day of meeting He sets. Until then, my heart is set on eternity, but I remain in His service. There is no other road to salvation, only Jesus, the Door. There is no boasting in this life except in the salvation purchased for me in Jesus alone. Nothing needs to be added to Jesus's gospel story. Boasting and arrogance are both serious offenses to God, and I made a choice to fear Him above all else in life. How about you?

Why do I even bring that up? It's mentioned here merely as a backdrop to what will be discussed.

Too many Christians and non-Christians, believers in Jesus and everyday people, are involved in spiritual mixture. We looked at the scripture before, but it is also relevant here:

> And if it seems evil to you to serve the LORD, choose for yourselves this day whom you will serve, whether the gods which your fathers served that were on the other side of the River, or the gods of the Amorites, in whose land you dwell. But as for me and my house, we will serve the LORD. (Joshua 24:15)

This is Joshua's mission statement, not a pithy plaque hanging over a door in someone's home. As a believer in Jesus Christ, the truth has, in fact, set you free. If you are a pre-believer and have not yet stepped across salvation's threshold, consider Joshua's words.

This mission statement encapsulates what the Lord Jesus expects: He expects you to choose. Jesus does not force anybody into a relationship with Him. He is not a spiritual manipulator or a salesman. Eager believers may have offended or caused you to feel spiritually accosted. It happens.

Nevertheless, Jesus is not at all interested in selling you anything. He offers salvation as a free gift—one you cannot beg, borrow, or steal to attain. However, He offers it to you with the caveat that you understand it is an *all-in* proposition. His Ten Commandments include the *command*, not the suggestion, that you have *no other gods before* Him.

The Lord does not hide His jealous, all-in love for you in the fine print so that you only understand it after you agree to His salvation covenant of marriage. No, He says it up front: If you marry Me, there'll be no extramarital affairs with other gods or idols as long as you shall live. Jesus is an eternal Spirit.

So why is it that so very many Jesus followers have committed adultery against the Lord? He cannot be unfaithful. I'll repeat that for you: Jesus cannot be unfaithful. His character is not built for that; neither can He act unfaithfully. Only you can act unfaithfully.

You have choices. God does not bind you into relationship. He asks and rightly expects you to remain faithful to Him. That does not give us license to break our covenant with Him. He cannot and will not ever do that. This is how His grace works. When we sin against our faithful "Husband" (Lord), He invites us justly to ask Him for forgiveness, and He gives it.

Okay, let's bite into the meat of this chapter, shall we? The devil is a duplicitous debonair debutant. What does the word *debonair* mean? In today's society, someone who is debonair is seen as charming, sophisticated, and cheerful. It describes a person you would never guess had an issue or care in the world. Believe it or not, when the Holy Spirit used this word with me, I did not know what it meant.

In this role, the devil hopes to remain unrecognizable to you until you are a pawn held tightly in his red-gloved grip!

Recognize then, that the devil, in this role, is difficult to detect, as he is primarily a deceiver! Duplicity speaks of playing all sides at once, so the devil does this in a charismatic way and in a splash of light as he makes his debut.

Let's unwind the lies together. Christians are often described as uneducated or needing a crutch by secular pundits. This includes actors, talk show hosts, newspaper editors, podcasters, university professors, politicians, authors, novelists, scientists, radio hosts, and most non-believers. We are not considered economically savvy or particularly "connected" by those who consider themselves trendsetters. We are just not as sophisticated.

> And many of those who sleep in the dust of the earth
> shall awake, some to everlasting life, some to shame and
> everlasting contempt. (Daniel 12:2)

Believe me, I have read a lot of articles, and these descriptors are just the tip of the iceberg that represents the many derogatory remarks hurled at believers. They truly see Jesus followers as idiots, and they scoff at us. Non-believers state these things in accordance with their own understanding and belief systems. Perhaps you, too, used to think as they do. But then you met Jesus, and now, you are happily dubbed an idiot if need be. You understand He is the Savior of your soul, and gladly own the title of "willing to be a fool for Christ"!

One of the most beautiful examples of this heart attitude toward the Lord, coming from misunderstanding onlookers, slides easily from the mouth of King David when he addresses his wife about his behavior before the Lord. While she was disgusted with him, he said this:

> I will be even more undignified than this, and will be humble in my own sight. (2 Samuel 6:22a)

Have you ever observed a snake charmer? Very often, the eyes of those absorbed in the practice of charming snakes begin to look like the creatures they are supposedly hypnotizing. Interesting, eh? What a perfect example—a snake charming a snake. The devil in this role charms us, producing in us an enemy of God, operating against God's ways and walking in the rebellion of sin. This is his primary object: to keep a person very much in need of redemption (from hell) from being swept into real life with Jesus, the Redeemer of all. The first death in the biblical description is natural death, and the second death ends in eternal life with Jesus or eternal separation from God in hell.

> Adulterers and adulteresses! Do you not know that friendship with the world is enmity with God? Whoever therefore wants to be a friend of the world makes himself an enemy of God. (James 4:4)

> To open their eyes, in order to turn them from darkness to light, and from the power of Satan to God, that they may

> receive forgiveness of sins and an inheritance among those who are sanctified by faith in Me. (Acts 26:18)

There are other terms that reveal the nature of the devil. They reveal who the saboteur genuinely is in your life. In this guise, he projects a certain sense of sophistication, refinement, or dash. He tempts you to entertain yourself with the "idea" that you meet all of culture's fine distinctions, and that they are better standards than godly or biblical ones.

Some time ago, the overtly sensual book, *Fifty Shades of Grey*, became a bestseller and then a blockbuster movie. In the lead character, we can see a flamboyant picture of both duplicity and charm; it was marvelously sketched in ink and elevated for all to "ooh and ahh" at in movie form. Many Christians I know not only read the book but bought it for their daughters as if it was some kind of important spiritual sexual epiphany. In reality, it only titillated their flesh, and they chose it over God and His Word.

Eroticism can be paraded before you as a higher plain of consciousness, but it will ultimately disappoint when those satisfaction levels cannot be maintained. Eroticism might be pleasurable, but it is still earthly and temporal. Jesus's kingdom is not temporal. His salvation satisfies forever.

The devil will flatter you and cause you to believe that you portray the best image possible. In arrogance over our own intellect, ability, agility, talent, dress, beauty—you fill in the blank—we can fancy ourselves above the need for a Savior.

It is the saboteur who congratulates us on our achievements and calls us a *self-made* man or woman. By saying this to our flesh, we erase God from the equation of who we are and anything we have accomplished. And no one can boast of that, truthfully. The belief that we orchestrated any piece of our life through our own hard work, determination, and discipline with no help from others is ridiculous. That doesn't describe anyone alive on the earth!

That train of thought says: I fought, bought, and paid for everything good in my life! I earned it! Why would I need some sappy, soapy religion? It's all a farce anyway. The last thing I want now is a religious experience. These are the thoughts formed in the dark heart of the saboteur and too easily absorbed by those who listen to him. Is this you or someone you know? Keep reading.

Manipulated by him, this person believes they "got there" all by themselves, and they fail to recognize that even the breath in their lungs was given to them by God. We actually belong to Him. Our eternal soul returns to Him (it's on loan for now), but our body will go the way of all flesh (try as we might to hold on to it). Each person will be judged by God at the end of our human life and given our reward based on the life we chose to cultivate with Him or within ourselves.

A refined individual, by culture's tally, is a person who is polished, honed, sleek, wealthy, sharp, and good on their feet. They have a ready wit and tend to reject those with a lack of personal discipline. They often believe their life is a well-oiled machine built for success, and not failure! They are clean, possibly sharp dressers, and may even be healthy eaters with toned bodies. They surround themselves with others who are like them—those who do not "suffer fools"—especially when it comes to Jesus.

It is a little bit comical that this same group of people often open themselves up to all kinds of nonsense: medicine-cart frippery, pharmaceutical baubles, Yoga retreats, and whatnot. They challenge themselves with hot Yoga, wear crystals, praise New Age practices, listen to gurus, and attend silent retreats with a yogi, seeking enlightenment. In like manner, they take part in chant worship to demons and try every newly touted body-bending, physique-shaping beauty regimen, but Jesus? Oh no! Please don't talk about Him. Jesus is the stuff of crazy town people!

If I am talking to you, the snake charmer, satan and his hordes of fallen ones have got a real harness around your neck.

This idea of being dashing describes a thrill-seeker—one who never met a challenge they couldn't, or didn't, conquer with aplomb! Do you consider yourself an adventurer of adventurers? In fact, do your adventures never cease? Do you race around the globe looking for the next one? Am I saying that seeking adventure and being a happy traveler is a sin? No! Not at all!

The earth is full of God-designed wonder on display! Many adventures await you. The question pertains to the Source for your life. Are you really running from Jesus? When will you stop and consider Him? Hopefully, before His second coming! Each of us needs to stop and consider why we are alive. It is a philosophical question on one level, but it's far more a spiritual question. It has a spiritual equation with a simple answer. Jesus is coming again, and chasing adventure perpetually without Him at the helm of your life is folly. It holds no meaning whatsoever. It is enjoyable. It is pleasurable. Many experiences are both, but to what purpose?

Spiritual mixture is a slow suicide. It is self-sabotage.

An eternity awaits you with that question still lingering. Who will you choose to spend it with? The saboteur of your life, forever separated from your Maker? Or with Jesus, the loving, ever-living Architect of light, healing, joy, peace, and wonder you can experience daily in a deep and lasting relationship? He leaves that decision to you.

It is important for us to be aware of this, not only for our own benefit, but for others so we can help them to know the one true God.

You shall have no other gods before Me. (Exodus 20:3)

Spiritual mixture is a slow suicide. It is self-sabotage. It looks like a hodgepodge of gathered belief systems, all stuck in one place, without any one rising to the top of one's consciousness. Many of these people feel proud of themselves, or wiser than others because they've curated these supposed treasures and brought these varied practices into their life. They think it makes them special. You'll see this a lot with well-traveled people. They are not always the Bohemian types either, but often, the well-educated university graduates with degrees and doctorates. However, it can also be your average soccer mom or baseball-loving dad. Whatever the category, spiritual mixture will lead to their destruction and not their edification.

How does the saboteur influence such a person? Satan's character traits are listed in God's Word. It covers the entire world of darkness he seeks to bring into your life as he attempts to steal, kill, and destroy. Spiritual mixture allows for three arenas. Let's look at it in case it describes any area of your life.

Let's visit one of the most succinct scriptures in which Jesus Himself outlines the saboteur's most blatant categorical traits. We'll go to John chapter 10, verse 10. Perhaps you've read it before and ho-hummed your way past it, saying, "Yes, yes I know," as an avid churchgoer, or perhaps it's brand new to you. Either way, it is as my father, used to say about a matter: "You are looking at its white-hot nuclear core!"

We find three spiritual life-threatening traits of the evil one as described by Jesus, our Good Shepherd. Here he gives an analogy of two types of shepherds who are polar opposites of one another.

> The thief comes only to steal and kill and destroy; I came so that they would have life, and have it abundantly. (John 10:10)

Steal

This *thievery* comes in the form of *highjacked spiritual objectives* that were given by the Holy Spirit to each living person who seeks out God, and their purpose is revealed as they give themselves to Jesus. Think of the saboteurs in the Civil War who tore up steel and railroad ties, put explosives or impassable debris on the tracks to keep supplies from reaching the other side's troops, be it weaponry, food, or medical supplies. This happens in modern day and spiritual warfare all the time. It is a time "dishonored" methodology of that ancient serpent. Think too of disenfranchisement as it comes to robbery. The deceiver alienates, marginalizes, defrauds, or otherwise manipulates outcomes so the believer will not be successful or as successful as they might have been.

Satan in this form always maintains the "hireling" or the false shepherds attitude, as John's Gospel points out. The meaning of this statement is vital if you are to understand what the Word is *revealing to you spiritually*. The liar shows up in the form of a caring shepherd or sidles along, pretending to be mollifying, but his heart is ever that darkest black. He is false, fake, an actor, duplicitous in all his ways. We have been told many times that for a lie to work, it has to contain some truth in it. The dragon is an ancient expert at such a role. Beware Christian, beware. Take great caution non-believer, as this one will first of all seek to keep you from ever knowing Jesus. He does not want you to have Jesus-believing friends or go to a church or a Christian concert, and he'll manipulate situations to get you in with a boss or a professor or a friend group that mocks and ridicules Jesus followers. Awaken to this old, tired, wearisome tactic.

Kill

What is gravely serious here is the Christian who takes this lightly. What is written is not meant to strike inordinate fear but rather wisdom in your spirit, and thus your actions. When John wrote that the enemy comes to kill, he was extraordinarily honest. The Holy Spirit will never trick you or lie to you. Do not take the fact that the wicked one wants to murder you for granted. That may sound dramatic, but it is nonetheless truth from the mouth of One who cannot lie. Before you can ever get to that altar to confess your sin to a prayer team, before you ever darken the door of a church to hear the life-altering message of the gospel, before you meet that friend on the college campus who reveals to you a new and better way, the slippery snake will arrange every circumstance to your detriment. Actually, "to your detriment" is not harsh enough, so the Gospel writer, by the unction of God's Holy Spirit, says it outright: The saboteur wants you dead! *Well that sounds harsh; he doesn't even know me*, you might be thinking. That is why God's Word is so very lovingly precious. God knows him and kindly warns you without being ambivalent about it. Take the Lord's Word with complete sincerity. John 8:44 gives us further insight that backs this trait up with a bow on top, saying satan was "a murderer from the beginning." As was said in the 70s when I was growing up, "Get it? Got it? Good!"

Destroy

You might ask, what's the difference between *kill* and *destroy*? They seem the same to me, right? Wrong! The nuance in word usage is very well worth leaning into for understanding right now! Have you ever heard of the phrase "total war" as it relates to a military strategy? To explain, picture Nagasaki, Hiroshima, Atlanta burning, Serbia, Croatia, the aftermath of Vesuvius or the Big Island of Hawaii all around Moana Loa, or even Rome under Nero. What do each of these visuals or textbook historical examples recall? If you do not know, it is *utter devastation*!

When the Lord comes to judge those who are completely rebellious and God-rejecting in the end, one of the His names describes Him as *a Consuming Fire*. This isn't child-book sweet, nor is it the same as the saboteur. This is God, in His *righteous judgment* toward those who chose to follow satan completely, giving their eternal soul to him.

When satan pursues a person for destruction, he goes "scorched earth" policy! There is nothing comical, cute, or funny about him. You have only to read the book of Job in the Old Testament to see how far satan will go to re-orient one human life toward himself in order to get him or her *to curse God and die*! Many face-plant on the "plains of hesitation" or in the "valley of confusion" or "mountains of doubt" when they *are pursued with satanic fury*, or as one old gospel poet wrote, "the hounds of hell."

Satanic traits are real, and devilish intrigues are persistent. The serpent's ways are deadly and thorough as they are given into. The point is not just to kill you, but to wipe out legacy, hope, your life's work, creativity, your Christian witness, your reputation, and your mark on a generation. He works relentlessly to get the mightily-used influential Christian to fall with gusto—with embarrassment so he or she will never stand up again! The diabolical effort is *to erase* any imprint of light you have made and to discourage you from ever thinking to unfurl from your fetal position if you have fallen from great heights in the Lord's work or in the secular world's eyes. The best thing a fallen believer can do in such a circumstance is repent heartily and meaningfully. There is no half-effort nor duping God. Think about King David in 1 Samuel after Nathan the prophet pays him a visit. Go read it now. Place yourself in David's shoes and follow his godly example. There will be epic fall-out (consequences to sin), and you must bear it. However, know this, it is FAR BETTER to fall into the hands of God than *to relinquish your eternal soul to the devil.* Hell is no place to go. You should wish its destination on no one! Tell the saboteur, "Not today, satan!" We must do this with humility and with *repentance* and *contriteness of heart, mind, soul, and body!* Run and do not walk into the Father's arms with Jesus's name on your lips, by the power of the Holy Spirit!

Subterfuge is a key ingredient in any spiritual mixture. What is *subterfuge?* It is an evasion of truth; something intended to misrepresent the true nature of an activity. It is deception.

Now that we've covered a variety of aspects concerning this ugly trait, let's examine how this spiritual issue might appear in a believer of Jesus. It is hard to imagine that this could be true of even older Christian churchgoers or staff members, but it is. Remember, the saboteur is a duplicitous debonair debutante, so he manifests this in a haughty, arrogant, judgmental, know-it-all spirit.

This is a sophisticated spirit, which you may have heard called a Jezebel spirit. This spirit manifests rebellion against God, which is the sin of witchcraft (1 Samuel 15:23). Anyone in long-time ministry has met this spirit. Unfortunately, it often shows up in females, though that is not always the case. I have personally experienced this demonic spirit hundreds of times inside churches all over the world.

Upon entering relationship with Jesus at the point of salvation, we enter a serious and joyous marriage covenant of faith. We stake our faith (our full trust) in Jesus, and He gives us His name in exchange for our old life. The full benefits of this union include an inheritance with Him and the seal of the Holy Spirit, marking us as belonging to the kingdom of light, understood fully by every dark spirit who sees it in the spirit realm. It declares, like a stamp of love, "This one is mine!" The seal of the Holy Spirit is not like a tattoo. Our body decays over time and is no more. This mark, or seal, is spiritual in nature and is permanent, eternal.

Perhaps a picture will help give a deeper understanding. After salvation, many pick up their former worldly suitcase filled to the seams with sinful behaviors and practices, and bring it into the church body. Being discipled or mentored in their new life in Christ by a seasoned, more mature believer should always occur. When this does not occur, barely a hair of change is noticed.

When you come to Jesus, it is a "come as you are" prospect for sure, but it is not supposed to be a "stay as you are" trajectory. My husband, John, came up with this great illustration: The new believer brings that packed bag right on down the center aisle of the church, and with no transformative mentoring in the Word, worship, baptism, or practical discipleship, a not-so-curious thing happens. After having lived life in the darkness of the world, with no checks on any of their practices, behaviors, or habits, that individual will bring unwanted change to the church's spiritual climate, especially to a young, immature body.

However, the sin of pride has no place in the kingdom of light. When you leave the kingdom of darkness, you have chosen to exit the saboteur's grip. You have repented of your past life and practices that you now know did not please your Maker. Then you hold fast to the Good Shepherd's hands and walk in His ways. It is not your way *plus* Jesus's ways. It is not your way *with* Jesus's ways sprinkled in either. He does not want to mesh with your former philosophies of life. It is His way. Period. I cannot imagine lecturing the mechanic about my car's inner workings, which I know nothing about, but we do this all the time with God and call it a day.

No, we need to find life in *all His ways*, not religiously, but because we realize we *need* Him. We also recognize that He knows better than we do and is fully trustworthy! No one expects a person to empty their spiritual closet in one night, of course, but choosing not to recognize and embrace God's change at that juncture is foolish. The sinful things you practiced before you got saved are not conducive to growth in the kingdom of light. Pride is a characteristic of the saboteur, not God, and pride is on display whenever you choose self-will over His ways. We cannot afford to keep sinful, occult, or lustful garments in our spiritual closet. Salvation is a surrender—a good one—to a Savior who already proved He loves you with the full extent of His love.

We cannot afford to keep sinful, occult, or lustful garments in our spiritual closet.

We must not reach for the benefits of the kingdom of light while still practicing darkness or attempting to hide the fact that we still dabble in the kingdom of darkness. This does not fly, as my late father, an ex-pilot, used to say. Doing that tells God that you trust yourself to lead your life more than Him. When you genuinely accept Jesus as your Savior, you need to acknowledge that being your own savior was a big deficit to you. You are not God—He is. Write that on a sticky note, and put it on your mirror for a while if it helps you. You are a creation of God, but He is the Creator of you!

Humility is the substance of the kingdom of light. The only light in heaven emanates from the Lord. Pride is an unnatural, unwelcome element in the kingdom of light, and it cannot abide with the holy light of God. The only thing upon which one boasts in the kingdom of light is Jesus!

How does a Christian remedy the problem of pride? Water baptism is meant to be the first symbolic practice of your newfound faith in Jesus. This occurs following your choice to acknowledge Jesus as your Savior and Lord. Many people have taken a step to accept Him as Savior, but have never, ever made Him their Lord. To make someone your Lord, you choose a position of humility and submission to their greater authority. The waters of baptism are a reckoning with the fact that you are sinful and in need of cleansing from the world.

Unfortunately, many believers have not understood the critical role water baptism is meant to play in setting a Christian up for success. Many of those choosing to come to Jesus, who have then followed with water baptism, did not realize that water baptism is really an altar. It is an altar of sacrifice where you die to selfish desires, sin, the flesh (lust, power, greed), and choose to mirror your life after Jesus instead. In this altered place from your previous life, you are now a child of light, and you learn to walk His walk and talk His talk. This new walk and new talk occur authentically, not religiously. Water baptism is where your pride is killed off.

When pride even attempts to arise, and it will, you hit it with a fire-hose of "Step back in Jesus's name! Pride is a killer of faith in Jesus.

Real humility is a genuine understanding of what Jesus has done for us, positionally speaking. It is a supernaturally born, divine eruption within your soul that causes a complete about-face to the world and its ways.

Once we are saved, we do not reach for the devil's toolbox anymore. Those old tools will not work in the kingdom of light. God has no need of them, nor does He want them in His body.

God does not see those old ways as sophisticated, clever, smart, or wise. He purposefully calls them foolish, dung, fodder to be burned, an abomination, etc. Wow! Those are strong words. God even says He hates those things. They have no place in God's kingdom, so they have no place in His body either.

> These six things the LORD hates, yes, seven are an abomination to Him: a proud look, a lying tongue, hands that shed innocent blood, a heart that devises wicked plans, feet that are swift in running to evil, a false witness who speaks lies, and one who sows discord among brethren. (Proverbs 6:16-19)

When we put on the devil's garb and follow his direction in our life, his wicked counsel is to mimic him and act like him. My husband put it this way: "They are like dressed up players in a fancy casino, wearing a gown or tuxedo." The duplicitous debonair debutante beckons us to gamble away our life! He entices us to live our life to be *seen*—to get all we can by taking what isn't ours by any means and then showing up to do it all over again. But ultimately, it's just a façade.

Water baptism is where your pride is killed off.

He leaves you feeling empty, not full; seen, but not satisfied; winning, but never enough; amassing all we can, but never complete. This leaves you in a place of futility. The book of Ecclesiastes gives an accurate depiction of this situation in which the saboteur traps us. In the end, Solomon described a man who had everything but was hollow, empty, and dissatisfied within.

The devil will do his utmost to be sure that's exactly how we land. By this point, he has been waiting stealthily and patiently like a big cat in the bush watching for its next meal, playing the long game. The killing blow eventually comes. He never deviates from his true nasty character. The finish line was always synonymous with our destruction, so let's steer clear of him and his designs.

Take some time in prayer and tell God in what ways these pages shone light on any dark stuff in your life that you no longer want to live with. Give it to Him humbly. If you are a believer, but recognize yourself in this chapter as having backslidden into some of your "old man" habits, repent now. He loves you.

> If indeed you have heard Him and have been taught by Him, as the truth is in Jesus: that you put off, concerning your former conduct, the old man which grows corrupt according to the deceitful lusts, and be renewed in the spirit of your mind, and that you put on the new man

which was created according to God, in true righteousness and holiness. (Ephesians 4:21-24)

If you have ever read C.S. Lewis's *The Screwtape Letters*, you will be aware of this strategy: If I can't get him one way, I'll get him another way! The saboteur will make use of your unchecked arrogance and see it as an entry point or foothold to hoist himself into your life. He'll use your religious legalism in a church atmosphere to wound other believers and pre-believers, as well as you! However, if the Holy Spirit is pricking you right now, repent. Legalism is not spiritual growth, but a spiritual hindrance under the influence of the saboteur! Listen to the voice of the Holy Spirit. He will guide you into the truth you need to know in Jesus, and cleanse you through the power of His Word. Prayer and maybe even an accountability partner will go a long way in helping to disentangle us from this gambit of the evil one.

Chapter 9

Beautiful Pretender

The devil and his demons can see the potency in the lives of godly men and women to determine those who are strong threats to them. When they try repeatedly to destroy your success in following Jesus, but cannot seem to defeat you with frontal assaults, they move on to different methods in their efforts to eradicate one whom they perceive to be their future foe.

> So she [Delilah] wove it tightly with the batten of the loom, and said to him, "The Philistines are upon you, Samson!" But he awoke from his sleep, and pulled out the batten and the web from the loom.
>
> Then she said to him, "How can you say, 'I love you,' when your heart is not with me? You have mocked me these three times, and have not told me where your great strength lies." And it came to pass, when she pestered him daily with her words and pressed him, so that his soul was vexed to death, that he told her all his heart, and said to her, "No razor has ever come upon my head, for I have been a Nazirite to God from my mother's womb. If I am shaven, then my strength will leave me, and I shall become weak, and be like any other man." (Judges 16:14-17)

This approach appeals to the most basic level of our heart—intimacy. The enemy hopes to eliminate the source of our great strength entirely, just as he finally did to Samson. Samson's soft spot was turned on him, and it became a target for the beautiful pretender.

This crafty—and shapely—tool has the capability to obliterate kingdom work, top to bottom! It is cleverly positioned to try to thwart God's plans. The enemy wants to bring about the full collapse of what God has built to reflect His glory. We can get so caught up in our own stories that we forget we are here to represent God's kingdom. We are not just here for our own pleasure and fame. Samson's story was a lesson in fumbling the ball through an old-as-time stratagem. We call it sleeping with the enemy—that wily, old serpent.

His attack is three-pronged. For one, he strikes anyone God is raising up for His glory (or in Samson's case, Israel's victory). He is bent on bringing about the destruction of that person through adultery (defined as sexual or spiritual infidelity), and to do this, he sets them up to implode. In the end, they collapse with a pancake effect, like a building being razed. Have you ever seen footage of this? Explosives are so strategically placed that a huge tower can be destroyed with shocking accuracy, and without disturbing the place next door to it.

This also occurs from a spiritual perspective when the beautiful pretender has slithered into our life, and we've given him full access. He can approach us in the form of impure sexual habits, addictions, false friendships, lustful entanglements, and more. In an instant, he can destroy us—our reputation, our work, our witness, and most of all, our family life. This combination is oxygen paired with fire for anyone in ministry, so watch for it, and root it out wherever it exists!

This strong spirit is completely debauched and pulls at our flesh. We cannot overcome it alone. We need to get accountability partners if we sense that we are not just struggling with our own flesh on this issue. We have to overcome it before it swings through our life like a wrecking ball. Otherwise, the damage released will result in an unholy mess, so we must pay attention and resolve the issue without delay.

This is a warring, relentless, seducing spirit, bent on turning our affections away from God. Prayer and discernment are key. If you see this in your wife or husband, talk with them and pray with them. This is a strong spirit that seeks to control and entice, so fight it off. It is also good to enlist other prayer partners to intercede for you in that effort. (Of course, only include people who have proven their ability to keep matters concealed to the prayer closet. Never trust a gossip!) These spirits are sent to capture and bring down their targets—most often powerfully and uniquely gifted men and women.

In Samson's case, you'll notice that he was not a fully submitted man and was far too cavalier with his tremendous gift of physical strength. He also had a negligent attitude toward the enemy; he went back and forth with Delilah as she constantly tried to kill him, but he shrugged it off anyway. In time, the saboteur blew them apart!

You can overcome these spirits by enlisting God's perfect, wise, and timely good counsel. His Word is the weapon for this battle; it is the sword of the Spirit (Ephesians 6:17). We are not dealing with human flesh, but an entity that has been playing this wicked, successful, and unholy game for years! Whatever you do, do not engage with it. Instead, unseat it by the power of the Holy Spirit!

Think of pride as a highly flammable liquid fuel that supercharges every character flaw we possess.

Samson did not look like a strong man for the kingdom of God. No, he did not! Let's rid ourselves of that religious picture right now. Samson has often been incorrectly depicted in children's Bibles as a tall man with bulging muscles. It is easy to understand how artists got there. However, the real muscles Samson possessed were not achieved through human effort or some great workout regimen; they were God-muscles! They were not built in an ancient gym where Samson trained daily. These

God-muscles were not obvious to the human eye. Nonetheless, they were there.

God sent Samson to save Israel from the trouble they were in! God doesn't need our muscles to make His work effective. If you are disciplined in prayer and fasting, that is great, but they are just personal disciplines that prepare you better for God's work. Always remember, God is God all by Himself.

Wondrously, we are the blessed recipients of His holy work, but we must not forget and think that by our muscles, our strength, or our ability we can accomplish anything. If we go down that road, we will be trapped in our pride and will have opened ourselves up to attack.

Think of pride as a highly flammable liquid fuel that supercharges every character flaw we possess. We must shun this unholy attribute along with any pull we sense within us to use deception to achieve anything. Pride is like tar, sucking us down like quicksand. Pride is the diabolical essence of the beautiful pretender. It was the issue behind his rebellion in the first place. He wanted to be God and thought himself equal with Him. But he wasn't, and he isn't.

God is our all-in-all, and He co-partners with no one! We are His beloved and useful human tools in His utterly capable hands. If we think we are more than that, we need to think again. If you see pride within you, and we all do, we need to fight the good fight and lean on the enabling power of the Holy Spirit of God to deal with it. He has given us all kinds of tools: prayer and fasting, time with Him and in His Word, honest fellowship, and much, much more.

We are part of a large family. We can find help from this trusted group of godly friends who wash themselves in God's Word. The Holy Spirit readies us to help one another in prayer and intercession on our behalf to God. These methods will help us join forces to defeat the very real foe attempting to assassinate every one of us.

Don't make the mistake of handling it on your own. Many have and failed miserably. We need each other, and we definitely need help defeating this foe and forever removing his footholds. As we humble ourselves before God and confess our pride to one another, God deals with this and helps us.

But let's get back to Samson. Why did the enemy feel the need to take Samson out? Let's look at that very closely. It was Samson's cavalier treatment of God's gift to him that opened him up to attack. It put him in a place he should never have been. God called Samson to a life of holiness, but he did not choose to follow it as he should have. Instead, he visited harlots.

Do you have places like this that you visit? On your phone? Or some-place you frequent? We are surrounded by these places—businesses, websites, fallen people. We need to stay away! Let God be our GPS (God Positioning Satellite). Samson's parents tried to guide him and were hard-pressed to get him to listen to their better judgment with regard to his choice in women. It was always about women with him. We'll call it the Delilah problem.

Delilah is the embodiment of the beautiful pretender! Be aware that "Delilah" doesn't always come in female form; she can shapeshift into whatever we desire, so in this way, the enemy fashions our specific brand of poison. That is his evil gift. The devil is a gifted groomer, as we see on full display in the agents of human trafficking all around the globe. He is a soul-trampler. But that is for another book!

The Holy Spirit gives us discernment so we can identify any seduc-tive influences that come to tear us down. Those forces want to rip to shreds that which was meant to glorify God. The devil attempts to break apart God's kingdom. Let's not disappoint or thwart the glory God wants to reveal in and through us! We need to be vigilant, recognizing the work of the beautiful pretender before our hard labors for God come crashing down!

Samson's case is notable in that it clearly shows how this method destroyed him. Samson was an enormously gifted individual who was sent by God to save a nation, but the devil used Samson's own errant feet to walk him into Delilah's lair. This scenario is all too common. Choose not to go this route.

Use Nehemiah's strategy—born through his avid prayer life—to avoid this.

> But we prayed to our God and posted a guard day and
> night to meet this threat. (Nehemiah 4:9 NIV)

Nehemiah posted a physical guard, and we can too. What does that look like for us, spiritually speaking? We need spiritual guardrails; prayer and a strong accountability structure will actively combat the devil's plans.

Remember, he is a hungry, roaring lion who wants to devour you. He is never full—just perpetually hungry! The only thing left when lions are done feeding is bones. Gory though it may be, a visual is what helps us best. God's Word paints necessary pictures like this for us so we will act in accordance with the actual threat level in front of us. He would not have us ignorant of the dangers around us.

We as a church, as Christ's body and bride, have been underestimating the saboteur's expertise and bearing the penalty for our lack of understanding and vision. We need those guardrails more than we know. It is vital that we protect ourselves through our own prayer life, as well as honest relationships with trusted people who will call us to account. If we travel, we should not do it alone. Travel with your spouse every time you minister, and if you are single, take a believing friend who is also a prayer warrior. We must help one another in this area.

The primary issue is our thirst. Where do we satisfy our thirst? Which well do we dip into? Stop and ask yourself that question right now. Where do you get life-giving, life-sustaining spiritual water? You have a choice, as there are different kinds of wells:

> Therefore with joy you will draw water from the wells of
> salvation. (Isaiah 12:3)

> Understanding is a wellspring of life to him who has it.
> But the correction of fools is folly. (Proverbs 16:22)

> The words of a man's mouth are deep waters; the wellspring of wisdom is a flowing brook. (Proverbs 18:4)

> As a fountain wells up with water, so she wells up with her wickedness. Violence and plundering are heard in her. Before Me continually are grief and wounds. (Jeremiah 6:7)

> These are wells without water, clouds carried by a tempest, for whom is reserved the blackness of darkness forever. (2 Peter 2:17)

This issue involves the same mixture we studied earlier. We sometimes think we can dip into another source, other than God, for refreshing—without any consequences. At first, it may seem that way, but it doesn't end there. There is a point of conviction here. And we should be responding appropriately to God's conviction by turning from these wells and not getting into them more deeply. Watch out that you do not justify sin. This is a specialty of the beautiful pretender.

When you have internal arguments with yourself to justify your dates with Delilah, it is a red light indicating that what's going on in us is not just fleshly, but demonic in nature—or both. Stop your internal arguments with the Holy Spirit! He is the One who has been at work helping you. We know instinctively that God would intruct us to run from Delilah—leaving our coat behind and never looking back—just as Joseph did in Genesis 39.

During these internal conversations, many have become accustomed to telling themselves that they deserve to dip into other wells because they are exhausted from serving and working so hard. We need rest (which is true) or a restorative moment (which is also true). So the enemy uses our needs to beckon us toward him, promising to satisfy us—but he doesn't.

We don't need to be going to these other wells. They are not restorative or refreshing. Instead, they are specifically and expertly fashioned for our demise. Their waters are not sustaining and do not offer the eternal substance found in God's well of salvation. So watch and pray, and do not drink from other wells.

This is a very serious problem in the present day. We often ascribe our fleshly desires completely to ourselves and do not recognize the way the enemy tries to exert his forces in those areas too. It is wise to recognize the destructive and entangled pathways that can lead to our downfall.

If the Spirit of Truth is speaking to you right now, stop and ask Him to reveal the truth of your heart to you. He knows if you need a "pull the fire alarm" moment! Trust Him to help you, because He can.

It is wise to recognize the destructive and entangled pathways that can lead to our downfall.

If you are a believer, ask the Holy Spirit to empty every evil thought that is not from Him. Tell Jesus that you give the enemy no place and no authority in your mind, heart, or body to manipulate you. Ask the Holy Spirit's voice to come through the demonic haze and reveal to you if you have been doing this.

Do not let the saboteur unseat you by these means. Above all, do not let him hoodwink you into removing the candlestick of the glory of God that you hold (Revelation 2:5). You hold this candlestick as you labor for God's kingdom of light. He wants to use you for His glory. To do that well, we should wait on Him through prayer and specific petition, so that if there is any issue for us in the future, we can deal with it, root it out, and continue onward for His glory and name's sake (Romans 3:21-26).

> For it is God who works in you to will and to act in order
> to fulfill his good purpose. (Philippians 2:13 NIV)

Don't let the devil hijack a restorative moment for you. We want to be whole and well for the service of the King. That is what this is about and nothing more. And since we are earnest in our service, we do not want to be ignorant of the devil's devices. He labors to stop our progress through bait-and-switch methods. Once the bait has been set and we've bitten, we are hooked—until we ask the Holy Spirit to remove those hooks from our flesh in Jesus's name, by Jesus's blood, and through Jesus's authority which He gifted to us. Take the Lord up on His glorious offer!

The beautiful pretender is just that—a fake. He is an exceptional pretender, but there is nothing truly beautiful about him. He is the foulest being we could ever imagine, and his true appearance would appall us. Nevertheless, he deceives entire nations:

> For by your sorcery all the nations were deceived. (Revelation 18:23b)

If he has ensnared you, put in a hotline call to God now! It is a spiritual emergency. His traps are real and meant to annihilate you. Don't kid yourself. The saboteur is completely evil and has been at this destroying work for a long time. It began with his fall from heaven, and now it is playing out on earth. You are not immune. You must battle it. You have tools to use against him that are deadly to him, but don't tell yourself that you are too smart to fall. That is a lie that comes from demonic influence, and we must tear down every lie of the enemy (2 Corinthians 10:2-6).

Earlier we read Isaiah 12:3, and we were instructed to lean in and drink from God's good well. Using God's dipper to drink from His well strengthens and empowers us.

I recently heard a prayer warrior say, "The church is looking for a Jezebel spirit (open demonic rebellion and witchcraft), but we are encountering Delilah (personal attacks and seduction) instead." If you are not familiar with either of these biblical accounts, please read them right now. They can be found in 1 Kings 18–19 and Judges 16.

This situation isn't accidental but by demonic design. As believers, we have got to stop thinking that the enemy of our soul is stupid (Matthew 10:16; 2 Corinthians 11:3). In these verses, his methods are not being praised, but exposed. It is important that we see his devices for what they are, instead of letting them remain cloaked by his deception!

His devices are not new; he has been using them for centuries on every generation. As you discover them, you will be able to recognize and combat them with your God-given spiritual weaponry—not your brainpower or self-will. Those human tools are useless against a foe who is spirit and not flesh. We are not up to that task, but God is.

We must not let anyone put a roadblock in front of the Holy Spirit's work in us.

Even in his spirit-state, the saboteur is not all-powerful, nor has he retained his original heavenly intelligence as Lucifer (Isaiah 14:12) Only God is all powerful and all knowing! If we remain teachable and use the tools made available to us by the Holy Spirit, we are indomitable. Our authority and anointing are from Jesus Christ through His empowering Holy Spirit (Philippians 2:13). God is far more powerful in His ability to take territory for His kingdom than we have ever imagined or witnessed! Again, this is not about our personal authority exercised through our own strength, but the authority we have because Jesus purchased it for us when He conquered sin and death.

We have the Holy Spirit within us to help us do this. Additionally, we must hold fast to the truth found in God's Word. We must not let anyone put a roadblock in front of the Holy Spirit's work in us. If you are a believer but have never been baptized in the Holy Spirit, ask Jesus about it! Ask Him if this Holy Spirit baptism is for you today. Ask the Holy Spirit to baptize you with His empowering enablement to do as the early church did! Ask Him and keep asking Him, just as the early church followers did. He will do through you exceedingly, abundantly more than you can ask or even think (Ephesians 3:20).

> Very truly I tell you, whoever believes in me will do the
> works I have been doing, and they will do even greater
> things than these, because I am going to the Father.
> (John 14:12 NIV)

Relationship is central to our faith. The temple curtain was torn from top to bottom—not because God the Father wanted us to have a relationship with people in our church or with a pastor—but so He could restore *His* relationship with us. This connection is vital. It brings us into union with God the Father, God the Son, and God the Holy Spirit according to His design. Therefore, we must be sure that it is built on God's Word and reject the false doctrines and idealogies of men. Only by being grounded in the Word and connected to Jesus can we do this.

And we must be on guard because false teachings have permeated the body of Christ. How do we respond to those we see? Sometimes in our efforts to not tear down beloved and trusted teachers, pastors, and evangelists, we say nothing, even when they are wrong. Anyone can veer away from Bible-based principles—usually because they don't understand them.

As a result, we have heard and experienced a powerless and diluted form of the gospel's empowering message. Indoctrination into mistaken beliefs rather than God's truths is common in our time. Meanwhile, God's richest benefits have been withheld from us. Again, much of this was not intentional by those leaders but came about because they received false teaching and chose to believe it over God's Word. The weight of peer pressure (the fear of man) operates—even in the church. God wants it gone!

The presence of God's glory evicts demons. That's right. Demons have been lying to us and trying to convince us that God's power and authority are not for us—or worse, they no longer even exist today. Cessationism is the belief that the Holy Spirit no longer uses people to perform miracles, and He no longer gives the gifts described in Acts 2, 1 Corinthians 12, and Ephesians 4. Adherents of this idea believe all that has ceased. However, the Bible does not agree with this ungodly denominational teaching.

It tells a totally different story, and God's Word is truth from cover to cover! We can trust His truth and be like Peter. He was not a learned man, but he had been in the presence of Jesus and followed Him by example. He went on to shatter the gates of hell with his testimony of Jesus. We are no different. Just like Peter, we are filled with the Holy Spirit and baptized by Him, so we can do just as Peter, the fisherman from Galilee, did. We can love God's Word and have a solid prayer life while learning to live very intentionally as a Jesus follower.

Indoctrination into mistaken beliefs rather than God's truths is common in our time.

Peter was not a teacher or a preacher, but God used him to take down the gates of hell, including idol worship inside and outside the church. He targeted covetousness of all kinds—for money or strength or position—and threw it to the ground with great power. Did someone tell you that you could not do the same? Do you believe that? Did someone tell you that you could not be like Peter or any of the apostles in your own time? Trace the ideas you believe to their source. If they do not line up with the Bible, don't listen to them.

We must take care not to heed people simply because they hold a religious position. They can also be influenced by demonic agency, and if another force worked through them and mediated away the power of Christ's Holy Spirit to you, who do they really work for?

Is there spiritual power like Peter's, Paul's, Timothy's, and Philip's in your church or community or family? If not, why not? Because there should be.

Remember, if you can be convinced that the Bible is not truth for you in some areas, you can be convinced it is not truth for you in others too. This is done by demonic orchestration through faulty Bible teaching. Not surprisingly, this problem is found in seminaries and doctrinal statements, as well as in the cultural appropriation of spiritual truths.

No doctrine should trump God's mighty spiritual weaponry. It was because of Jesus's disgust over such practices going on in His day that He flipped tables! First and foremost, God's house is to be a house of prayer! The above-mentioned doctrines of men are not of God and are contrary to His plan for His people, but these demonic influences have infiltrated the church. The Bible tells it plainly:

> And in vain they worship Me, teaching as doctrines the commandments of men. (Mark 7:7)

> "Do not touch, do not taste, do not handle," which all concern things which perish with the using—according to the commandments and doctrines of men. (Colossians 2:21-22)

> How much better to get wisdom than gold! And to get understanding is to be chosen rather than silver. The highway of the upright is to depart from evil; He who keeps his way preserves his soul. (Proverbs 16:16-17)

The beautiful pretender is intent on his mission, so he certainly will not stay out of the church. Since he understands the ways we want to fit in and tend to follow each other, he uses other well-meaning, *Jesus-believing* travelers to persuade us to go in the wrong direction. To this very point, Isaiah wrote:

> Listen to Me, you who know righteousness (right standing with God), the people in whose heart is My law and instruction; do not fear the reproach and taunting of man, nor be distressed at their reviling. (Isaiah 51:7 AMP)

So let's not check our brain at the door! Let's check our brain—and beliefs—with the Word of God. It is God we wish to follow, and God we want to worship, but we are easily turned. In a conversation with an angel, the apostle John was rebuked because he began to worship the angel after receiving the revelation he was sent to give. The angel said:

> Don't do that! I am a fellow servant with you and with your brothers and sisters who hold to the testimony of Jesus. Worship God! For it is the Spirit of prophecy who bears testimony to Jesus. (Revelation 19:10 NIV)

Beloved, we must hold to the testimony of Jesus, worshipping God, understanding that the Spirit of prophecy is known clearly by the Holy Spirit who enables us to bear the testimony of Jesus. Allow the Holy Spirit to sanctify and empower you to complete all that He has planned for you to accomplish. This world needs everything Jesus intends for it before He returns. Each of us has been carefully placed where we are to do that very thing.

Allow the Holy Spirit to sanctify and empower you to complete all that He has planned for you to accomplish.

In Mordecai's prophetic words:

> Do not think that because you are in the king's house you alone of all the Jews will escape. For if you remain silent at this time, relief and deliverance for the Jews will arise from another place, but you and your father's family will perish. And who knows but that you have come to your royal position for such a time as this? (Esther 4:13-14 NIV)

The saboteur's work in this world will eventually come to an end. Meanwhile, he's been active in every generation, fostering and feeding on every avenue open to him—and he will continue to do so until this earth's bitter end—destruction.

Jesus said:

> But as the days of Noah were, so also will the coming of the Son of Man be. For as in the days before the flood, they were eating and drinking, marrying and giving in marriage, until the day that Noah entered the ark, and did not know until the flood came and took them all away, so also will the coming of the Son of Man be. (Matthew 24:37-39)

> Jesus answered them, "Do you now believe? Indeed the hour is coming, yes, has now come, that you will be scattered, each to his own, and will leave Me alone. And yet I am not alone, because the Father is with Me. These things I have spoken to you, that in Me you may have peace. In the world you will have tribulation; but be of good cheer, I have overcome the world." (John 16:31-33)

Jesus spoke directly to His disciples about the dangers He foresaw—*before* He went to the cross. They concerned Him then and now. He knew we would face evil, but He knew the Helper would be with us. Ask the Holy Spirit to show you the hour you are presently living in, so you will be aware of the real battle around you.

Be aware of the enemy's tactics; don't stop believing in Jesus because bearing His testimony has become "too hard." Don't accept any gospel other than the one you find in the Bible.

If you have wandered—each to his own place—and are not in the center of God's will, let Jesus speak to you right now. He promised that we could have His peace, regardless of tribulation. You may have experienced difficult trials in your past, or perhaps you are right now. Jesus says this to your heart: "Be of good cheer, I have overcome the world."

Jesus's words are not a Hallmark greeting set down in ink to make you smile for a moment. They are your life! They are what sustains you!

They are a deep wellspring that never runs dry! Write them on your walls. Post them around your house. Etch them onto your heart! These are not the words of a man, but of God. Every word Jesus speaks is divine and, consequently, life to your spirit every time you read it or hear it! Jesus's words are perpetually full of life. Think about this: Jesus is the Word, and everything was made through Him! His words are far deeper than time itself because they are sourced in eternity. You are meant to cling to Jesus's words every day of your Jesus-believing, Word-bearing, testimony-giving life until He returns or you are translated to your eternal home with Him!

Moses wrote this under the influence of the Spirit of God:

> Fix these words of mine in your hearts and minds; tie them as symbols on your hands and bind them on your foreheads. (Deuteronomy 11:18 NIV)

Chapter 10

Traumatic Trickster

Behold, I send you out as sheep in the midst of wolves.
Therefore be wise as serpents and harmless as doves.
(Matthew 10:16)

This chapter could have easily had the subtitle: But what about aliens? The reason it does not deal with aliens or ghosts specifically is because they are a distraction from the works of God. That is ever the saboteur's top priority. Do not forget that!

The devil uses and manipulates aliens and ghosts and the like to get our eyes off of God.

Through happenings of odd kinds, usually in our youth, we think we had a spiritual encounter. It often goes something like this:

"When I was eight, I saw (or spoke to or felt) a ______________ presence in the room with me. No one can tell me I didn't see it. It was real." Fill in the blank. People will place these unexplainable phenomena on the same level as their faith; it has simply been filed away in their mind.

I want to challenge you to clean house. If you have, even unknowingly, made a friend with a demonic entity at some point, that spirit will not want you to unmask it. One of the ways you will know if you have an issue in this area is by the way you feel when reading about it. Pay attention to your attitudes as we tackle this topic. If you find yourself becoming agitated, your repentance may be necessary. If you are not sure, you can ask Jesus if there is a dark spirit blocking you from God's truth. The Holy Spirit will reveal it to you. We need to relinquish any unsubmitted areas to Jesus and do the spiritual work of dealing with them to find healing.

Jesus wants to set us completely free from *all* worldly entanglements and anything that attempts to draw us back into its sway. Jesus acts as the Healer so we can be fully free! The enemy will always try to keep you in bondage. He wants your spiritual life stagnant so you can grow in his direction without any of the spiritual pruning from God that we need. No one is immune to the need for tune-ups. The Lord came to set us free so His peace can permeate every area of our life. The demonic tries to look like God, but that realm offers only darkness. God gives us life *in* Him led by *His* Spirit and filled with *His* gifts.

The demonic tries to look like God, but that realm offers only darkness.

If someone tells you that meeting and speaking to a ghost or an alien (or the feeling of any presence) was on par with meeting God, we have a problem! The traumatic trickster is deceiving them.

Why use the word *traumatic* in naming this chapter? Seeing a ghost or alien or angel can either be incredibly traumatic or it can feel warm as tea and cakes with a beloved family member. Often, these entities show up looking like deceased loved ones or friends (Leviticus 20:6-7).

> Give no regard to mediums and familiar spirits; do not
> seek after them, to be defiled by them: I am the LORD
> your God. (Leviticus 19:31)

When God tells us to keep out of some territory, we'd better listen! Don't do it! Stop and repent right now if you have. Ask for God's forgiveness because it is a sin to carry on in spiritual conversation with any spiritual presence except God. This practice defiles us.

God specifically tells us not to seek them, which denotes pursuit on our part. People pursue other spirits through many means, some obvious and others less so. They include tarot cards, seances, mediums, necromancy, trances, hypnosis or hypnotherapy, crystal balls, palm reading, astrological charts, the occult, witchcraft, wicca, the use of occult paraphernalia, the use of psychedelic drugs, channeling, Yoga positions and Eastern sexual practices, and the choice of demonic movies, music, and books to name only a few.

Are you "into" horror movies and books as a genre and indulge in them frequently? This includes any graphic novels or gaming with occult themes woven into its plotline. Be careful of the words you repeat in songs, or those that a video game declares over you repeatedly. These seemingly harmless things are not without occult power. They can harm you or open portals to dark presences that seek your harm. Pay attention to lyrics that sanction sexual perversion, demonic practices, summoning the devil, and calling out curses. This is only a thumbnail sketch to get you started, but it's important to find and root out things that will add spiritual trauma in your life.

The trickster, in his guise as an alien or a dead relative, is causing trauma, even if you think it's good. It's not. Jesus, on the other hand, is good; He is a Healer and deals only in truth. The saboteur is the destroyer. He will use trauma and trickery to trigger experiential worship of a detrimental nature. You may not worship the devil with dark rituals, but he will attempt, through trickery, to drain any worship you would have given to God by elevating that which is demonic in nature. He will use mystical or mysterious experiences to get you to believe that these are as valid and solid as any real God-encounters you may have had. God has no equal, and time with Him cannot compare.

So if you are talking with Grandma regularly when she died years ago, or obsessing over the sight of an alien in the forest you saw when you were eight on a camping trip with your uncle, stop. Take those experiences to the Holy Spirit and let Him sort it all out. Take the control back from the saboteur and hand it to Jesus who gave Himself for you!

Remember, it is Jesus who brought salvation through His death on the cross. He paid the price for us. He made a way where there was no way. Shut the mouth of the traumatic trickster and celebrate the God who loves you and has claimed you as His own.

The saboteur can only take what you willingly give him, and he fears Jesus. There is no other name under heaven or under the earth that strikes more fear in the demonic realm than the name of Jesus. Jesus's blood gave us hope. Because of Jesus's sacrifice, we can spend eternity with God and not be locked out of heaven in a Christless hell. We must take care of our spiritual life.

So what about aliens? The trickster delights in getting us sidetracked or obsessed with literally anything of a spiritual nature—anything except Jesus. Anything that possesses a spiritual presence other than God's power is demonic. All associates of the saboteur are off base for us. When we focus on the dark realm, we are giving our time and allegiance to it, and this is a form of worship to something other than God.

Heavenly realms—the realm about the Earth's atmosphere—is the area demonic beings are said to occupy. Their goal is chaos; they want to disrupt the plans of God, and steal, kill, and destroy God's creation, especially people, God's greatest treasure. The highest heaven is God's home where He and His heavenly hosts dwell. When Jesus was born, they came right into the domain of darkness over the earth and announced His birth to the shepherds with great joy. They were not one whit afraid to occupy that space for their mission. There is no place God cannot go. He is the deed holder of all the earth and all the heavens. No other being compares to God in power.

The story of Peter walking with Jesus on the Sea of Galilee is related in Matthew 14, Mark 6, and John 6. Jesus calls Peter to come to Him after Peter requests to walk to Jesus upon the waves, and this happens:

So He said, "Come." And when Peter had come down out of the boat, he walked on the water to go to Jesus. But when he saw that the wind was boisterous, he was afraid; and beginning to sink he cried out, saying, "Lord, save me!" (Matthew 14:29-30)

Think of a magician for a moment. They distract you in some way, so you miss the clever, little details they use to perform their trick. Similarly, the saboteur uses the unexplainable and the mysterious to keep people enthralled. He does not care how he takes your mind off of God, as long as he does take your mind off of God. Don't be a victim. Be victorious!

Chapter 11

Lover of Self

Only God fills the role of Savior! *Yahweh* is His name!

In the course of time, Absalom provided himself with a chariot and horses and with fifty men to run ahead of him. He would get up early and stand by the side of the road leading to the city gate. Whenever anyone came with a complaint to be placed before the king for a decision, Absalom would call out to him, "What town are you from?" He would answer, "Your servant is from one of the tribes of Israel." Then Absalom would say to him, "Look, your claims are valid and proper, but there is no representative of the king to hear you." And Absalom would add, "If only I were appointed judge in the land! Then everyone who has a complaint or case could come to me and I would see that they receive justice." Also, whenever anyone approached him to bow down before him, Absalom would reach out his hand, take hold of him and kiss him. (2 Samuel 15:1-5 NIV)

Sounds like a politician, doesn't it? Absalom behaved like this toward all the Israelites who came to the king asking for justice, and in this way, he stole the hearts of the people of Israel. Are you like this? Are you a lover of self? Many believers get defensive on this point. This is not simply a problem for spiritual people. This is an issue for the entire human race!

Self-love is not bad. It's when self-love trumps love for God that the problems start. The devil knows this, so he disguises it as a good thing, a right thing, a pursuit we should manifest all by ourselves—without the help of God. The word *manifest* has become a buzz word lately. If you are "self-realizing" or "manifesting," what do you need God for? Get that tricky saboteur language out of your faith life now!

Manifestation of self comes from evil realms, not God-realms, and it is demonic. If God wants you to have something, He does it through your cooperation with His Holy Spirit and in unison with His will for you. You do not accomplish anything by yourself with God in the second seat after you. No. He is always first and always leading. Humility is key in a Christian's life. Humility cannot be faked. God is a holy God who created and loves you, and He knows our true condition.

> **You do not accomplish anything by yourself with God in the second seat after you.**

Absalom had it going on, as they say. He was a king's kid, just like so many who have grown up in the church. Absalom was extremely handsome. Partially because of his father, he was an influencer. Would people have loved to know him if he had not been the king's son? (Just asking for a friend.) Not likely. His charm might have given him an audience, but not like being the offspring of a powerful, God-established king did! Absalom was cool. (We know what that looks like today, don't we?) He had an audience, allowing those with grievances to bypass his father, King David's authority.

The "gate" today would be any place complaints are discussed: the city center, a place of business, even your workplace, church, or gym. Choir rehearsal and Sunday school class could come into this too.

Absalom collected stories and feigned *a greater care* for the people than his father, David, seemed to be giving those with grievances, gripes, complaints, and concerns. Absalom listened. He knew how to manipulate friendships and ease the mind of the troubled, and he sought to elevate himself over his father while sitting at the gate of his father's own kingdom!

This spirit is pervasive. Absaloms do not have to be male; they can take a female form too. The perceived efficiency of such a one puts them on a "what would we do without you" footing. Any individual who walks the way of self-love projects the saboteur's self-love to the disenfranchised in a church, business, or other setting.

Are you an Absalom? Let's look at the fruit this spirit produces.

Absalom's self-love wrought division, undermined God's chosen man, betrayed his family, pitted family groups against one another, acted politically to unseat his own father, disregarded God's choice for the throne of Israel, and considered his own position higher than God's will and way. As a result, he created a plan to wreck his father's house, which eventually brought about his own demise and demoralized the entire nation following his death.

Can you spy any godly characteristics that would justify an Absalom spirit? Anyone who sways hearts to leave God's camp and choose their own plan instead of God's is of satan. Some claim to follow Jesus but intend to set up their own power base. They are entranced by their own beauty and position. Their perceived importance is their true priority, not the love of God. They are operating from demonic territory.

The apostle Paul warned the early church in Galatia to not "use your freedom to indulge the flesh." The word for flesh is *sarx*, which is the sinful state of human beings not governed by the Spirit of God. Paul went on to say:

> If you bite and devour each other, watch out or you will
> be destroyed by each other. So I say, walk by the Spirit,
> and you will not gratify the desires of the flesh. For the

flesh desires what is contrary to the Spirit, and the Spirit what is contrary to the flesh. They are in conflict with each other, so that you are not to do whatever you want. But if you are led by the Spirit, you are not under the law.

The acts of the flesh are obvious: sexual immorality, impurity and debauchery; idolatry and witchcraft; hatred, discord, jealousy, fits of rage, selfish ambition, dissensions, factions and envy; drunkenness, orgies, and the like. I warn you, as I did before, that those who live like this will not inherit the kingdom of God. (Galatians 5:15-21 NIV)

This actually says that anyone practicing these things will not inherit the kingdom of God! It's a serious issue! So look at the list and pray over it right now. Does any of it describe you or something you struggle with? If so, these things will not want to go out of your life easily, not if they have been fostered and have lived there for a while. It may take some real deliberate time to work with the Holy Spirit to expel it all, but you will have freedom as you invite the Holy Spirit to make you into His person, one who operates to please God! Keep at it until you receive the full victory in Christ!

Paul also wrote this:

Since we live by the Spirit, let us keep in step with the Spirit. Let us not become conceited, provoking and envying each other. (Galatians 5:25-26 NIV)

Christ dwells in you! Think about that. You are His habitation, and His Holy Spirit *lives in* you. That means the fruit of the Spirit that you see in Galatians 5:22-23 are your essential roommates. When you let the fruit of the Spirit truly live in all the rooms of your life, the other roommates will not be able to abide their presence. However, the opposite is also true. So take a moment and consider your fruit. Let's take stock of ourselves as lovers of God and not self.

Chapter 12

Consummate Pickpocket

The law of first mention says that the way a word or idea in the Bible is *first* used lays a foundation that the Word will continue to build upon. It describes the saboteur as "crafty and wily," so that makes this the most important thing God wants us to know about satan. *Arum* is the Hebrew word used here, and it translates as "shrewd, cunning, crafty, wily, or sly." Its root word, *aram*, means to be slick, bare, or smooth. In today's speech, we call a deceitful person "a smooth operator" and consider them "slick." Satan is much more dangerous in this guise than he is as the roaring lion.

The longer a deceiver can go undetected in our life, the worse the damage he can inflict. As soon as he "outs" himself, people tend to be far more watchful. Although he adores the spotlight, he is rarely revealed as he really is. Instead, he uses something from his closet of disguises.

He is a smooth talker. Psalm 5 speaks of those who operate like this:

> Not a word from their mouth can be trusted; their heart
> is filled with malice. Their throat is an open grave; with
> their tongues they tell lies. (Psalm 5:9 NIV)

The Orthodox Jewish Bible says something very informative:

> There is nothing trustworthy in their mouth; *their inwardness is a corruptible abyss*; their throat is an open [grave], they speak *smooth deceit* with their [tongue]. (Psalm 5:9 OJB)

Employing flattery and smooth deceits, satan cunningly contrives to upset God's plan. He wants to topple God's position and snatch it for himself to establish his own diabolical kingdom in its place. The kingdom of darkness mirrors his twisted image and corrupt ideas. It is this boiling craving and constant lust for God's throne that drives him.

His thievery began from the very dawn of time. A rip-off artist, he will steal anything and everything, claiming it all as his own. His blasphemies know no bounds. Driven by greed and envy, he is fully intent on his vile operations. The inner deception that he can do this motivates him in this unrelenting, wicked pursuit. So he sells himself to the people of the earth. It's obvious in those who listen to his counsel (Proverbs 12:20; Jeremiah 7:24).

At his wicked, inner core, the consummate pickpocket is siphoning people's worship and transferring it from God to himself in one way or another.

The minor prophet Nahum said this:

> From you comes forth one who plots evil against the LORD, a wicked counselor. (Nahum 1:11)

It can also mean: one who imagines evil against God.

It's important to note that while satan can imagine all kinds of evil all day long, it does not mean he can bring it to pass. Prayer thwarts the devil's schemes. As we pray using the Word of God and being guided by the Holy Spirit, these proposed "hatchings of evil" will be stillborn!

Hebrews 3 tells us to be alert, watchful, and on guard against developing an "evil heart of unbelief." We covered unbelief earlier, but what happens when unbelief takes up residence in our heart? We become susceptible to the very worst disease: apostasy.

There can be no more distressing moment in the life of a backslidden (apostate) believer than the fact that we can "depart from the living God." How terrible! For satan, it's the ultimate heist. Pause here for a moment to ask if you have fallen prey to this scheme. To prevent this state, the Word tells us:

> Exhort one another daily, while it is called "Today," lest
> any of you be hardened through the deceitfulness of sin.
> (Hebrews 3:13)

Let's take some time here. Are you in the habit of encouraging your fellow believers in Jesus Christ? This can be done in many, many ways. We are admonished to help each other. This is never a one-way street. No matter how poor you think you are or how difficult life is for you, there is always something you can give to another. Jesus is full of treasures to offer—sincere encouragement and Scripture can lighten the load. In this way, we help one another.

When we get stuck in life's ditches, we need help. In the same way, we should assist others. Help a brother. Help a sister. It's vital that you be led of the Holy Spirit in this. Don't let anyone drain you. We are all growing, and some are not as sensitive as they ought to be. If we are careful to be led by the Lord, it will all work out well in the end, but we need to follow Him obediently. Satan will happily pickpocket your time, talent, and treasure if you are not grounded in Holy Spirit obedience. Pay attention to these things.

To exhort is to encourage strongly. An exhortation should be Holy Spirit procured, meaning your words and actions are put before Holy Spirit *first* before you speak. That is *always* the best policy.

A hardening of the heart can come in when you walk in *trials* and *tribulations*, and instigated by the devil, choose to take things out of God's hands. Rebellion rushes in. This wayward behavior moves you away from God and His paths.

Imagine this: You're driving your car down an unknown and windy road in the dark during a raging storm (your trial). Just as you reach a bend in the road, you yank open the car door and shove God out of the driver's seat, simultaneously taking the wheel yourself. This isn't going to end well. Even though you somehow got around that bend where you left God, you're sure to meet with a flat tire—or worse, your first pothole. It's too bad that God is not in the car anymore, isn't it?

Don't blame Him. You used both feet to kick him out! The good news is that when we own our behavior and wrong heart stance to God, He can help us and restore a right attitude.

Instead, satan will come right into that situation with you on the side of the rode to blame God and convince you (because you opened the door to listening to him) that God has not been, nor will He ever be there for you. He'll suggest that God has abandoned you—not the reverse.

In one of the many ways he likes to offer something he cannot give, the devil loves to absolve us of sin. He loves to pat us on the shoulder as the pretend comforter, while he reaches into the pocket of God's designs, hoping to steal every bit of them from here on out. Refuse that burglar access right now!

If you recognize a pattern like this in your life, take some time and invite the Holy Spirit to show you anything specific you need to see. Spend time with God, and repent for any attitude or action the Holy Spirit has pinpointed. Deal with it, so his thievery ends today.

Exhortations prevent the *pickpocketing* that could happen daily to those who are unaware. We need to have each other's back. We are to watch out for one another with care, concern, and Holy Spirit intercession—not gossip, backbiting, and sabotage. Encouragement and exhortation are protections, specifically against an evil heart of unbelief, which leads to a departure from the living God. The deceitfulness of sin leads our heart astray and hardens it.

So today, as the Word puts it, put God on the top of your list, moving all else aside! God is well aware of every draining, life-sucking circumstance in your life that threatens to rob you of your inheritance in Him (Hebrews 4:7).

Put the consummate pickpocket on notice that the living God is alive in you. As you invite the Holy Spirit in and kick the devil out, you invite the softening necessary for your heart in every place where sin has made it unwieldy, unpliable, and proud before God. Push this heavy weight off the side of your vessel, and wake up to the destiny God planned for you even before your conception!

Sinister is an old word meaning "from the lefthand side." To operate with the left hand was thought to be operating in trickery or with malicious intent, or as "underhanded."

The devil's "sleight of hand" is very rarely obvious. He likes to keep his evil intentions to himself until he can strike a blow—to wound or kill. Sometimes, however, his intentions "bleed through," and the Holy Spirit gives us nudges to alert us. He is trying to point out the enemy's attempt to "deal you dirty"—that something underhanded is taking place.

Do not be lax or careless with the dreams and plans your Father has for you.

How often do we blow off such warnings? The Holy Spirit is faithfully doing His job—leading us into all truth and disclosing deception. Too often, though, we have not paid attention to His promptings. Instead, we have seen the slight upturn on the sides of the devil's mouth, or the glint in his eye—spiritually speaking—as we just turned a blind eye to God's leadings.

For some reason, we think we can *wish* these uncomfortable things away using our imagination, but we can't. Get used to taking these nudges to God, no matter how slight they may seem. Place them under the white-hot beam of God's eyes. He will not lie to you! Do not let the consummate pickpocket "wow" you—keeping you distracted by the harmless movement of his right hand, while he's actually carrying out the real plot with his left hand.

What God has given to you *belongs to* you. Guard what the Lord has given to you with the diligence it deserves. Do not be lax or careless with the dreams and plans your Father has for you. Remember, the consummate pickpocket will do all he can to edge you off your course in Jesus. Recognize the "doctored" moves this thief has developed, and call on God to deal with him by His authority and power, using your spiritual armor and weaponry.

Destroyer of Destroyers

> They had as king over them the angel of the Abyss, whose name in Hebrew is Abaddon and in Greek is Apollyon (that is, Destroyer). (Revelation 9:11 NIV)

The saboteur is an assassin with a catalogue of methods he uses to achieve his ends.

The saboteur is an assassin with a catalogue of methods he uses to achieve his ends. He does not possess creativity though. What some dub creativity on his part is simply the result of centuries of effort he has put into his evil craft. That is not creativity, it's cunning. Creativity begets life. The saboteur is all about death. Remember that. When you become familiar with his diabolical wares, you can thwart a good deal of the schemes and devices that have been set against you or others you love.

> The hired hand is not the shepherd and does not own the sheep. So when he sees the wolf coming, he abandons the sheep and runs away. Then the wolf attacks the flock and scatters it. (John 10:12 NIV)

Satan is looking to stir things up; he wants to wreck things.

> One day the angels came to present themselves before the LORD, and Satan also came with them. The LORD said to Satan, "Where have you come from?"
>
> Satan answered the LORD, "From roaming throughout the earth, going back and forth on it."
>
> Then the LORD said to Satan, "Have you considered my servant Job? There is no one on earth like him; he is blameless and upright, a man who fears God and shuns evil."
>
> "Does Job fear God for nothing?" Satan replied. "Have you not put a hedge around him and his household and everything he has? You have blessed the work of his hands, so that his flocks and herds are spread throughout the land. But now stretch out your hand and strike everything he has, and he will surely curse you to your face." (Job 1:6-11 NIV)

If you think this would turn out differently for you today, you are wrong. It wouldn't. If satan thinks God delights in you, you will quickly become his favorite target. Perhaps you feel like you already are, and you are trying to change that by reading this book.

> The LORD said to Satan, "Very well, then, everything he has is in your power, but on the man himself do not lay a finger."
>
> Then Satan went out from the presence of the LORD. (Job 1:12 NIV)

I have read this passage many times over the years, and I've always thought satan must have felt as if he had just been given the car keys so he could wreck it. You can almost feel the broil of rebellion and delight he gets from his presumed license in this situation. Clearly the devil no longer resembles what he was originally created to be. He is now completely foreign in nature to the pure, holy essence of God's character, which is full of light. The saboteur's nature, his outlook, and his unremitting goal is now broken, twisted, and hateful. Here you find an angry and aggressive spoiler eager for a fight.

Sometimes I think we read these Bible passages as though they are fables. We write them off as though the very real human tragedies and triumphs they describe didn't really happen, but that's not true. They aren't just good stories! Let's take away the teaching points and think about the complete malevolence behind what was happening to Job. How horrifying! We simply don't want to believe there is a real being who would think and do such things. Instead, we prefer to view him lightly as a fictional character. Because of this, the biblical narrative is of less value to us. We must never relegate God's Word to a tale or ancient lore.

The saboteur uses our words to throw a match on the gasoline-slick surface of those sins we habitually refuse to take to Jesus.

The truth is that Job was a righteous man who was sifted by satan in every way possible, short of taking his life. It's time to get into the nitty-gritty of God's Word! Job was a real man whose family members died tragically. Then, satan attacked him further. Take the time to read this epic volume told from the Holy Spirit's perspective through Job. The book of Job contains copious details about corrupted man, sin, arrogance, self-righteousness, God, identity, and His power and might, along with the insidious nature of a conniving foe set on destruction. Job also had some rather interesting friends who did not serve him well. Still, Job fought hard and sought hard through it all to honor God.

Even so, the destroyer of destroyers attacked him in many ways. One was through words.

> The tongue also is a fire, a world of evil among the parts
> of the body. It corrupts the whole body, sets the whole

course of one's life on fire, and is itself set on fire by hell.
(James 3:6 NIV)

The things that come out of our mouth can do real damage, and that includes gossip, malice, slander, backbiting, lying, false testimony, boasting, blasphemy, and sinful jesting. This kind of devastation is one of the saboteur's specialties. That's why James warns us about it. The saboteur uses our words to throw a match on the gasoline-slick surface of those sins we habitually refuse to take to Jesus. The enemy is a destroyer of destroyers. Words hurt people. Unlike the children's song, words can be used like sticks and stones to incur real pain.

They are a weapon of the evil one, who loathes our every breathing moment. Each of us should take stock of how we use our tongue. Read James 3 when you have a moment. We don't want to be pawns in the devil's hands. Instead, let's be Jesus's mouthpiece and a fountain of life!

Acts 8 gives some insight into another of the destroyer's attributes:

> Philip went down to a city in Samaria and proclaimed the Messiah there. When the crowds heard Philip and saw the signs he performed, they all paid close attention to what he said. For with shrieks, impure spirits came out of many, and many who were paralyzed or lame were healed. So there was great joy in that city. (Acts 8:5-8 NIV)

Philip performed many miracles. So did Peter and Paul, and that is a long, long list. After Jesus ascended into heaven and the Holy Spirit came, the miracles of God continued to flow, and they did not stop with that generation. In fact, they have never stopped, but they have been attacked. Unfortunately, that attack has had the ability to suppress them.

How could such a thing happen? Those who don't believe miracles still happen today have been *taught* to believe that way. This unbelief is a subject we've looked at before. Other *religious* men and women taught them to *not* believe. Jesus spoke about unbelief a lot. The religious leaders of His time were steeped in it. So Jesus dealt with it constantly. Do a word study on it sometime to see how Jesus dealt with it and what He thought about it.

The point is that this parched doctrine should be removed from the church. Instead, we can hold fast to our belief in Jesus and all He gives us: repentance, salvation through the cross, and a restored relationship with the living and powerful God. We can enjoy the assurance of sonship and the certain promise of eternal life, in addition to the outward signs of His inward work through the gifts and fruit of the Holy Spirit—and through *miracles*.

And what's so important about miracles anyway? Let's read what Jesus said about the miracles He was doing:

> If I do not do the works of My Father, do not believe Me;
> but if I do, though you do not believe Me, believe the
> works, that you may know and believe that the Father is
> in Me, and I in Him. (John 10:37-38)

Miracles have a purpose. God's miracles drew masses of people to Him. How joyous it must have been to see so many people set free and made whole. Later, Paul wrote that miracles were part of his ministry.

> I persevered in demonstrating among you the marks of
> a true apostle, including signs, wonders and miracles.
> (2 Corinthians 12:12 NIV)

Miracles attest to the power and love of God for mankind as He chooses to bring help that no one else can. In his assault on God's people, the enemy has worked stealthily through religious spirits to teach lies and sow doubt. In his mind, miracles—the powerful signs to the power of God that they are—have to be stopped! As the destroyer, he is focused on our words and what we believe most of all.

Let's take a moment to marvel at the plan and power of God instead. Jesus died and rose again for us. He wants us to know Him as the risen and powerful Lord and Savior that He is. Ask Him to show you any way that you need to submit to Him, either in your words or your beliefs. You've got this! May you be encouraged to walk as a believer in every way.

Back to the miracles: It was also doubt and unbelief that prevented miracles from happening in Jesus's time (Mark 16:14). What we believe really affects our faith. If we decide that Jesus can't heal, we are believing the doctrine of men over God. The Bible says He does heal. If we believe He does not do miracles, the Bible disagrees.

For the past several decades, the church has witnessed an open assault—even at the seminary level—in this area. Such faithless teaching is not in line with the Word of God. It is the work of satan through those wishing to elevate themselves and their supposed knowledge over the deeper understanding of what the Holy Spirit, who animates the living Word, says.

What kind of gospel have we received if it merely recounts the miraculous but has no power?

And there's more to it. The ridiculous notion that Jesus cannot heal today is a direct result of believing that Holy Spirit baptism is also not real and no longer occurs today as it did in the early church. It's heartbreaking to consider that many from that time and through the centuries gave their lives so the church (the body of Christ) would grow and thrive. They wanted it to be alive and full of vitality to this very hour.

No one wants to look Jesus—or any of the saints, prophets, or martyrs—in the eye and tell them that the sacrifice they made so we could pass along this golden thread of life did not matter. We need to look at what we believe. Who told you this? It was not Jesus or His Holy Spirit, or any of that large crowd of witnesses that has gone before us.

What kind of gospel have we received if it merely recounts the miraculous but has no power? Jesus never meant for us to wistfully read about the miraculous and not engage in it. He knew His power would be made manifest in every one of His followers as they had need. That's why He came in the first place. Jesus is the great I AM, the Resurrection and the Life, and that's the truth. Let's live like we believe that!

Some mock those who believe in the baptism of the Holy Spirit. They infer that these are not stable and must look for experiences and feelings. This is an unkind misunderstanding.

In Matthew, Jesus spoke about the demeaning labels that the religious leaders of His time tried to foist on John the Baptist and Himself. He concluded with these words:

> Wisdom is justified by her children [works]. (Matthew 11:19b)

> Wisdom is justified and vindicated by her deeds [in the lives of those who respond to Me]. (Matthew 11:19b AMP)

> Wisdom is shown to be right by its results. (Matthew 11:19b NLT)

What kind of results was He talking about? Jesus loved to heal and deliver people from demons in His ministry. Jesus loves to heal and deliver people from demons today too. Let's reread the end of that passage from Acts 8:7-8 in the Amplified Version:

> For unclean spirits (demons), shouting loudly, were coming out of many who were possessed; and many who had been paralyzed and lame were healed. So there was great rejoicing in that city.

What a marvel it is to read about this! But remember, the Bible isn't a storybook filled with fairy tales. These stories are here to remind us that Jesus is the same yesterday, today, and forever (Hebrews 13:8). Let the Bible build up your faith that Jesus is Savior, Healer, and Deliverer by the power of His Holy Spirit today! Imagine the rejoicing—not just for those who had been healed, but those who witnessed each life no longer bound by the destroyer of destroyers. Let's be a living church, as they were, despite our culture's dismissal of that power! This is our directive from Jesus:

> Jesus came and told his disciples, "I have been given all authority in heaven and on earth. Therefore, go and make disciples of all the nations, baptizing them in the name of the Father and the Son and the Holy Spirit. Teach these new disciples to obey all the commands I have given you. And be sure of this: I am with you always, even to the end of the age." (Matthew 28:18-20 NLT)

This is the Great Commission from the mouth of our Lord. Through His authority, we are to make disciples, baptizing and teaching them. Later, in Acts 9, we learn of Saul's healing and Holy Spirit baptism through the prophet Ananias.

> And Ananias went his way and entered the house; and laying his hands on him he said, "Brother Saul, the Lord Jesus, who appeared to you on the road as you came, has sent me that you may receive your sight and be filled with the Holy Spirit." (Acts 9:17)

That is quite the commissioning for Saul (Paul), don't you think? In Acts 13, on Paul's first missionary journey, we read this:

> When the Gentiles heard this, they were very glad and thanked the Lord for his message; and all who were chosen for eternal life became believers. So the Lord's message spread throughout that region.
>
> Then the Jews stirred up the influential religious women and the leaders of the city, and they incited a mob against Paul and Barnabas and ran them out of town. So they shook the dust from their feet as a sign of rejection and

went to the town of Iconium. And the believers were filled
with joy and with the Holy Spirit. (Acts 13:48-52 NLT)

The enemy hated Paul and incited a mob! He still does this stuff.
Here's an illustration. A precious young boy I know had just pitched a
fantastic game. In fact, it was his excellent pitching skills that had won
the game for his team as he had so many times before. He has a gift.
Following the game, a player from the other team slugged this precious
young boy's pitching hand.

We don't expect the unadulterated meanness of the enemy. We'll call
it anything else, but we refuse to call it out for what it is. Last time I
checked, envy was not a fruit of the Spirit. Neither is rage, nor covetousness, nor hateful destruction. The demonic seeks to work through the
flesh. The saboteur will never play fair.

When the light of your gifting shows (and it is for Jesus's team that
you do your finest work), you are going to be immediately targeted.

This is why putting on the full armor of God is not a suggestion, any
more than following the Ten Commandments is. Knowing what spiritual weaponry to use—along with when and how to use it—is vital for
every believer who wants to be effective. A person can possess a sword
and have no idea how to wield it. This fits far too many in the body of
Christ today.

Some of us have been told that our sword should "stay in its sheath"
through sermons that do not highlight the Holy Spirit's power. We're
told there's really no need to use the Word of God in our time. We've
been told that all the work has been done, which is only partially true.
Partial truths are the saboteur's most fine-tuned labors, sown into the
"hive-mind" mentality of many who are not awake to his work. Do not
be fooled!

Christ Jesus commissioned His disciples into real service. Jesus said
it is finished because He'd done the pioneering groundwork; without
it, we can do nothing. However, He fully expected and challenged His
church to take ground, not relinquish it.

All of Psalm 37 is powerful, but let's read verses 11-15:

> But the meek shall inherit the earth, and shall delight themselves in the abundance of peace. The wicked plots against the just, and gnashes at him with his teeth. The Lord laughs at him, for He sees that his day is coming. The wicked have drawn the sword and have bent their bow, to cast down the poor and needy, to slay those who are of upright conduct. Their sword shall enter their own heart, and their bows shall be broken.

Do you see what the wicked want to do to the poor and needy—particularly the upright? The devil is at the heart of it all.

Jesus said that the devil was a murderer from the beginning (John 8:44). Jesus didn't mince words about the devil's character and intent. He chose those words accurately. The church needs to wake up and stop ignorantly partnering with the adversary to be part of the destruction of other people—believers and non-believers both. The devil delights in using people's words to hurt others and in keeping people trapped in unbelief. He does both simultaneously.

> Instead, you yourselves cheat and do wrong, and you do this to your brothers and sisters. Or do you not know that wrongdoers will not inherit the kingdom of God? Do not be deceived: Neither the sexually immoral nor idolaters nor adulterers nor men who have sex with men nor thieves nor the greedy nor drunkards nor slanderers nor swindlers will inherit the kingdom of God. (1 Corinthians 6:8-10 NIV)

> Do not be deceived: God cannot be mocked. A man reaps what he sows. (Galatians 6:7 NIV)

We will bear the fruit that we sow, so if we choose to believe false doctrine, we will bear its fruit. If we adhere to doctrine that is not in God's Word, no matter where it is from, then we are no longer following

God's Word. Period. So all ideas must be tested against how they line up with the Word of God. Whatever the source, be it a college, seminary, well-known teacher, or a blog you follow, we must be careful over what we believe. We want to be like this guy:

> A [discerning] king who sits on the throne of judgment sifts all evil [like chaff] with his eyes [and cannot be easily fooled]. (Proverbs 20:8 AMP)

The Word of God is our strong tower. It exposes the enemy's plans as well as his demise. What a mighty gift the Bible is for those who have ears that will listen, eyes that will see, and hearts seeking the Holy Spirit's guidance. Psalm 49 describes the demise of the saboteur and all who go with him in his way, in just a few lines:

> This is the fate of those who are foolishly confident, and of those after them who approve [and are influenced by] their words. Selah. Like sheep they are appointed for Sheol (the nether world, the place of the dead); death will be their shepherd; and the upright shall rule over them in the morning, and their form and beauty shall be for Sheol to consume, so that they have no dwelling [on earth]. (Psalm 49:13-14 AMP)

Therefore, it is vital that we are following Jesus and not "another" spirit that would pull us in the polar opposite direction from the path of life. There are not many paths to God; there is only one.

Thankfully, God does not withhold the essential things we need to know to keep us safe from the snare of the fowler. He helps us.

> For You will not leave my soul in Sheol, nor will You allow Your Holy One to see corruption. You will show me the path of life; in Your presence is fullness of joy; at Your right hand are pleasures forevermore. (Psalm 16:10-11)

God understands our hardships. The Psalms show that. When we are struggling with enemy oppression or see darkness at work in our life, read this psalm. It is the heart's cry of one who understood your plight and lived there. Oppression often hits hardest when God is trying to bring correction to us. The psalmist identified his affliction as God's wrath upon him, which is different in nature. The problem could be physical or mental, due to a rebellious heart issue, or something spiritual. In any case, God wants to help us with it. All Scripture is useful for these moments.

The Word of God is our strong tower. It exposes the enemy's plans as well as his demise.

Take the time to speak to God and tell Him you'd like to make it through your situation but need help. Make the choice to fear Him above all the other voices tugging and warring with your soul for dominance. Let Him lead you back to His good pasture! Sometimes we feel like this:

> Your wrath lies heavy upon me, and You have afflicted
> me with all Your waves. *Selah.* (Psalm 88:7)

There are few adults who can say they have never felt such an onslaught of the soul. Pray and use Scripture to get right footing in a Savior who loves you powerfully and seeks your healing and restoration, in full, not in part.

> Cast all your anxiety on him because he cares for you.
> (1 Peter 5:7 NIV)

Go to Him speedily. Never let another person, or a demon using a person, tell you that God does not care for you. He loves you! Remember, the devil only deals in death, but Jesus offers life.

To fear the LORD is to hate evil; I hate pride and arrogance, evil behavior and perverse speech. (Proverbs 8:13 NIV)

If you do what is right, will you not be accepted? But if you do not do what is right, sin is crouching at your door; it desires to have you, but you must rule over it. (Genesis 4:7 NIV)

The Father heart of God is evident in this verse when He is speaking to Cain. Before the murder of his brother, God saw what was in Cain's heart and warned him. He was telling Cain to reach out to Him. God saw the inner struggle of Cain's flesh, the temptations it produced, and the way they were overshadowing his ability to make right decisions. God sees that with us too. And He continues to reach out today, just as He did then.

Satan may not be suggesting you murder your brother, but he is suggesting something. He's constantly doing that. So let's be aware of his ways. He wants to use us to hurt each other and destroy our testimony at the same time, so don't let him. He steals your time through social media, entertainment, toxic friends that waste your time, and distraction after distraction after distraction. He will subtly try to shift your priorities, making social causes you care about more important in your life than God. Or he will get you absorbed in your love life, especially with individuals who do not love God. He does not care *how* he destroys your faith and testimony, just as long as it is indeed destroyed, along with you. So take a look at any way the destroyer of destroyers is active in your life through unbelief specifically.

Dear Jesus, where I have let other voices crowd out Your voice, I am sorry. You must be the One who guides me in all my ways and thoughts. You are my God. You have bought me at great cost to Yourself. Thank You so much. When I was on my way to hell and utter destruction, You came to be the Savior of my soul through Your death, burial, and resurrection. I renounce any and every way that I have misread Your love, discounted Your heart, or listened to other voices that did not tell me the truth about Your love and care for me. Forgive me for not nurturing my spirit, which You gave to me. I understand that through the Holy Spirit's work in me, I can rule over that which seeks to destroy me and my faith. I thank You for Your powerful Holy Spirit. Please guide me and keep me, my Redeemer and Good Shepherd. Amen!

Chapter 13

Monster Pet

And do not give the devil a foothold. (Ephesians 4:27 NIV)

Did you ever get one of those small "just add water" toys as a kid that enlarges to a far greater size from the minuscule gummy bear size it had been? As a kid, that's magical, wondrous fun, right? Seriously, this tiny little hard thing is now the size of a basketball! Amazing how it grew!

The saboteur does this too—only he is stealthy. He sneaks in as a monster pet in the form of people demonically manipulating you, habitual practices, idolatry, spiritual mixture of any kind, false doctrine, or extrabiblical teachings, to name a few. Of course he has a dangerous plan to keep taking over more territory—more than you can afford to give up. However, because this monster pet is wily, he'll move subtly enough to remain undetected if possible. Whenever he sees an inroad to take another swath of your "country," he'll take it. His pursuit often comes through familiar channels: a trusted friend, a family member, culture itself, institutions like churches or universities—ven entire states or nations.

He will never be content. Before long, he will have set up shop and have chained you to the wall in the back storage room of your life, having gained complete control!

That was purposefully worded to be uncomfortable to get your attention. It's very possible that someone reading this book right now has given up territory to that monster pet. He is the saboteur, and you must unmask him now! You've either opened the front door of your life and let him in with an actual invitation, or he has crawled up and over the back fence and made his way into the "home" of who you are. Again, any dabbling with the occult or contact with demons of any kind is a non-negotiable, no-go zone for God. He will not have or put up with any other "gods" in your life but Himself. When He comes, He fills us completely. Deuteronomy 6:4 says:

Hear, O Israel: The LORD our God, the LORD is one.

God will not live or cohabitate with the devil. He knows full well how damaging that monster pet is to us.

In this, we need a clear understanding of who God really is. That truth will help us to know not only the peril we can find ourselves in, but the power of the Lord of love who died for us.

God will not live or cohabitate with the devil. He knows full well how damaging that monster pet is to us.

God is completely holy and pure. He will not corrupt Himself with impurity of any kind. God is great, and He is full of love and mercy, as well as justice and holiness.

In the church, there are far too many spouting uninformed and shallow statements about God. Some sound like this: "Well, *my* God isn't like that." "I think God would be okay with that."

The truth is that God is God, and we are not. If we say something is from God, we'd better be able to back that up with His Word. We must not put words in God's mouth that He is not saying. You would not like it if someone did that to you.

Additionally, this is a classic move from the ancient, tattered playbook of the enemy. We need to walk humbly before God. If this idea offends you, go to God and ask Him to shine His light on your heart. You may have some unfinished business in this area. Put it before the Holy Spirit of God.

God will never fit into our small molds for Him. He is far greater than we could ever imagine, surpassing our greatest expectations. Whenever we need Him, which is all day and every day, He is there. This is a truth we grasp in increments as we grow in our relationship with Him. Our job is simply to genuinely pursue Him for who He truly is. He is magnificent and has a job so enormous that we can't fathom it. The justice area alone is daunting!

The vital point is that God is One. He cannot be separated into parts to suit some dashboard version of Him found only in our own mind. Jesus said this when asked which was the greatest of all commandments:

> "The most important one," answered Jesus, "is this: 'Hear, O Israel: The Lord our God, the Lord is one. Love the Lord your God with all your heart and with all your soul and with all your mind and with all your strength.'" (Mark 12:29-30 NIV)

Jesus is not a pet. Jesus is not an addition to your other gods and idols. He should not be mixed in with talismans, potions, Buddhas, crystals, or spiritual guidebooks. He is not a tiny god you can pocket for a day and bring out as the mood suits. Likewise, His cross is not there to enhance an outfit or dangle from your rearview mirror. The cross was an instrument of His death, where He demonstrated His enormous love for you! Jesus is fully God! So as your God, you can trust that He can teach you how to love Him, and He does.

When did we get the idea that we could shove God around? God's love for you is total. It's so complete that Jesus submitted Himself obediently to crucifixion on a Roman cross, carrying our sins, even though He was innocent of sin Himself. Those sins, placed upon Him by the heavenly Father, were forgiven for all, with no exception. He accepts all who believe in Him by faith.

Following that selfless act, the Bible tells us that His body was taken to the grave to conquer death (the consequence activated by sin). Again, Jesus never sinned, so He didn't stay in that lifeless place, but rose three days later, just as He said He would. He is a Word-Keeper. He is the Word made flesh. Jesus proved His love for us, leaving nothing undone! There is no greater love anywhere.

Jesus gave all of Himself for us and still offers all of Himself to us today. In exchange, He wants all of our affections too. He has no intention of sharing your heart with anything or anyone else.

He wants to be loved back—fully, completely, and with no reservation!

> ## Jesus gave all of Himself for us and still offers all of Himself to us today.

So don't say "my Jesus" wouldn't do that, and "my Jesus" wouldn't *limit me to Him alone.* Yes, He would! His Word stipulates that He measures love in words and deeds. He models this. He has shown His love for us through His Word and through His actions. Our goal is to live a joyful life of faith in which we reflect Him more and more in our ways, thoughts, and activities. We can do this through the living Spirit of God within us. Let's start knowing and loving Him well!

As we've seen, the monster pet is an aggressive intruder. He doesn't just break in. He breaks in at any time possible, and then grows there like an invasive weed! There are examples of this all over the world. Something not indigenous to an area quickly throws off the balance of life in the region, sometimes swallowing up unique plant and animal life that had existed as far back as anyone could trace! Havoc ensues.

The question is, what will you do about it? If you see a problem in this area in your life, don't go another day without dealing with it. Don't ignore it.

Hell is a real place, and the saboteur would love to have you join him there.

> Don't you see how wonderfully kind, tolerant, and patient God is with you? Does this mean nothing to you? Can't you see that his kindness is intended to turn you from your sin? But because you are stubborn and refuse to turn from your sin, you are storing up terrible punishment for yourself. For a day of anger is coming, when God's righteous judgment will be revealed. (Romans 2:4-5 NLT)

Repentance is a gift from God that brings us to the truth and will always tell us the truth. The monster pet and his motley crew will never do that because they want you floundering, tied up, or dead in the water. They want to use you, eventually becoming unmanageable. He is certainly not your friend. He only allows you to "pet him" in the initial days of your acquaintance to get you hooked on him, but he will never look like the monster he is at the start. Instead, he will come to you as a tiny gummy bear, just waiting for his moment to take over. We can only send him back with God's help. Jesus said this:

> Most assuredly, I say to you, he who does not enter the sheepfold by the door, but climbs up some other way, the same is a thief and a robber. But he who enters by the door is the shepherd of the sheep. To him the doorkeeper opens, and the sheep hear his voice; and he calls his own sheep by name and leads them out. And when he brings out his own sheep, he goes before

them; and the sheep follow him, for they know his voice. Yet they will by no means follow a stranger, but will flee from him, for they do not know the voice of strangers. (John 10:1-5)

May we follow only the one true Shepherd who died to save us.

Chapter 14

Pity Partier

If you are doing what is good, shouldn't you hold your head high? And if you don't do what is good, sin is crouching at the door—it wants you, but you can rule over it. (Genesis 4:7 CJB)

The saboteur is a liar. He will try to convince you that he will make you feel better, but he won't do it. He will try to camp out with you through your self-pity in "your house," which, if you are saved, is not your house but God's temple (1 Corinthians 6:19). He will encourage you to indulge your feelings and "follow your heart."

He [Jesus] went on: "What comes out of a person is what defiles them. For it is from within, out of a person's heart, that evil thoughts come—sexual immorality, theft, murder, adultery, greed, malice, deceit, lewdness, envy, slander, arrogance and folly. All these evils come from inside and defile a person." (Mark 7:20-23 NIV)

This is not a very pretty picture. We should never tell someone to follow their heart. What does the Word say about this?

The heart is deceitful above all things and beyond cure. Who can understand it? (Jeremiah 17:9 NIV)

The New King James Version says the heart is deceitful above all things, and desperately wicked; who can know it?

Jeremiah wrote by the power of God as the Holy Spirit directed him, like every other writer of the Bible. Jeremiah goes on to say this:

> I, the LORD, search the heart, I test the mind, even to give every man according to his ways, according to the fruit of his doings. (Jeremiah 17:10)

We make choices every day. We are being sold "a bill of goods" through our culture's influence. We can see it clearly in the music industry, the entertainment industry, on social media platforms, and in the constant marketing placed around us to lure us into any path but God's. Like a dog returning to its own vomit, we are being moved by the saboteur to make foolish choices:

> As a dog returns to its vomit, so fools repeat their folly. Do you see a person wise in their own eyes? There is more hope for a fool than for them. (Proverbs 26:11-12 NIV)

> It would have been better for them not to have known the way of righteousness, than to have known it and then to turn their backs on the sacred command that was passed on to them. Of them the proverbs are true: "A dog returns to its vomit," and, "A sow that is washed returns to her wallowing in the mud." (2 Peter 2:21-22 NIV)

> Their heart is deceitful, and now they must bear their guilt. The LORD will demolish their altars and destroy their sacred stones. (Hosea 10:2 NIV)

By following their heart, they began to practice other religions and were no longer following God. That is exactly what the saboteur planned and intended. He has set himself up to destroy you!

We don't want to be harsh, but we need to turn the lights on in our soul so the Holy Spirit can wash and cleanse us in this area.

God is all about healing. God is all about life. The devil only wants to make us sick in any way possible! He is leading people down a path to death. Nothing in the world can offer us true healing or true life. Only God can do this. Jesus said:

> My kingdom is not of this world…My kingdom is not from here. (John 18:36)

Speaking to the religious leaders of His day, Jesus said:

> You are from beneath; I am from above. You are of this world; I am not of this world. Therefore I said to you that you will die in your sins; for if you do not believe that I am He, you will die in your sins. (John 8:23-24)

> I have told you now before it happens, so that when it does happen you will believe. I will not say much more to you, for the prince of this world is coming. He has no hold over me, but he comes so that the world may learn that I love the Father and do exactly what my Father has commanded me. (John 14:29-31 NIV)

Mark these words. In them we can find the fragrant scent of life emanating from God's kitchen. God offers us supernatural, life-giving food for our soul. If we imagine His Holy Spirit of Truth facing off with the enemy of our soul, you'd better believe there will be an epic tug-of-war! As a result, satan will come after us from every conceivable direction to keep us as his victim.

So let's not fall for the saboteur's tired old traps. This is his *modus operandi*. Nothing new. And it is rotten to its core! When the party is over, and the lights are turned up on his garish show, the pity partier's "dance floor" is slick with death—stinking, putrid, and stale. We need to get off his merry-go-round of abuse immediately, once we identify it for what it is.

The saboteur doesn't want to comfort us, and he will not ease our pain or settle our heart. Only God loves us. As always, the saboteur is seeking God's place in our heart. Don't buy it. Only God provides true solutions and total healing.

The pity partier can only *pretend* to do these things. He is the god of this world, and he hates you. So to keep you in his corner, he offers catchy songs sung by the beautiful people in the entertainment industry to sully your soul.

The truth is that as our spiritual health develops and matures, it overflows into every area of our life!

However, once we know God, those songs sound different than before. We begin to examine lyrics and critically think about the social media gurus and podcasters. Are they really the "guiding lights" we thought they were? Do we want to spend time listening to the opinions of cultural icons in sports, music, academia, and even religion without asking the Holy Spirit if what they are saying is really nourishment that will build us up spiritually? The truth is that as our spiritual health develops and matures, it overflows into every area of our life! Praise God!

When we intentionally disconnect from the old pity partier, he will no longer have the inroads he once had. He will not be able to whisper in your ear like he did with Gollum in J.R.R. Tolkien's *Lord of the Rings* trilogy. Gollum was constantly tormented and torn between two masters. We need only one Leader and Master—God, and He has given us His Holy Spirit to lead and guide us. He can be trusted because He is all that is noble, pure, good, and true. He is always working for our edification, never tearing us down. God offers true wisdom.

> For it is written: "I will destroy the wisdom of the wise;
> the intelligence of the intelligent I will frustrate."[9] Where
> is the wise person? Where is the teacher of the law? Where
> is the philosopher of this age? Has not God made foolish
> the wisdom of the world? For since in the wisdom of God
> the world through its wisdom did not know him, God was
> pleased through the foolishness of what was preached to
> save those who believe. (1 Corinthians 1:19-21 NIV)

What a marvelous, eternal truth! God was pleased to save any who would hear Him and accept His pure offer of salvation, and He simultaneously gives us the power to help others find their way to Him too! Many times, our lives get hacked. The enemy has gained unauthorized access by illicit means, which we sometimes ascribe to God instead. The pity partier works to convince us that God is not good. Instead, we begin to think He is religious and hateful toward us and doesn't want us to be happy, successful, or loved.

This is a very immature and skewed view of God. It's like dinner from a microwave—quick and ready but not very tasty. The enemy sows these ideas in your heart and mind so that, in time, he can steal away your purpose as he destroys the idea that God even exists.

But wait a minute! The true and manifest God of heaven and earth won't just "go quietly into the night." No, He will fight for us! Nevertheless, we live in a mass of lies.

Even parts of the church worldwide are rife with denominational schisms and hypocritical sinful behaviors. On top of that, there's been a pagan takeover of organized religion that has turned away from following the Bible. This "religion" is like Marxism or Communism in that it is just another empty philosophy, just another ideology to follow, that is bereft of God's power and majesty. In this fashion, people think they can dispense with God. How sad.

---

9. See Isaiah 29:14.

Of course, our relationship with Christ is *ordered,* not organized. Organization suggests that is can be done by men, but a true relationship with Jesus is ordered, indicating that it is predestined and ordained. God supervises this plan, establishing our purpose and giving our lives meaning in the process. Why engage in anything in life that isn't ordered? By extension, why listen to anyone, religious or not, who does not have their life ordered by God?

The hallmarks of a life ordered by God begin with a relationship with the Father through Jesus as expressed through His Holy Spirit. From within our heart, He leads us in His grace, building a love for His Word and a strong prayer life. A believer loves others and strives to live at peace with all people. This lifestyle is radically different from what the world offers us.

The world believes that chaos and misbehavior are somehow fun. Is that because it comes at someone else's expense and not their own? That's not even true. Everybody loses in this arena, not just the injured party. Even so, the world is restlessly spewing ungodly deceptions on a daily basis, and the saboteur is the one behind every one of them! Jesus said this:

> You belong to your father, the devil, and you want to carry out your father's desires. He was a murderer from the beginning, not holding to the truth, for there is no truth in him. When he lies, he speaks his native language, for he is a liar and the father of lies. (John 8:44 NIV)

Jesus warned us about him because He wants us to understand what is going on. Jesus would not have us ignorant. So whenever you see any way that he has lied to you and led you into his dark paths, stop! Refuse him any further access to your future. Choose eternal life with Jesus instead.

> Jesus answered, "I am the way and the truth and the life. No one comes to the Father except through me." (John 14:6 NIV)

There is one way and one God. But the devil tricks people into thinking there are many routes to God. That is a lie. There is only one carrier providing the service we need to travel to Jesus—and that is faith in Him by His grace alone. Simple faith.

Pluralism, the idea that there are multiple ways to reach God, is taught in higher education systems today. I think they are getting lower and not higher! This reflects the worst education that could be offered to a human heart in need of a Savior. Unfortunately, many dysfunctional denominations teach the same thing.

Pluralism is a name for the divisions born in the heart of satan. These represent a diffusion of what was originally intended, as revelations from God are now all fenced up and labeled for only a few. This powerful insight was given through R.D. Bullock, but written in my own words. So the devil uses all of these cleverly devised myths to entice us away from simple faith in Jesus and the truth about our future with Him.

> Praise be to the God and Father of our Lord Jesus Christ, who has blessed us in the heavenly realms with every spiritual blessing in Christ. For he chose us in him before the creation of the world to be holy and blameless in his sight. In love he predestined us for adoption to sonship through Jesus Christ, in accordance with his pleasure and will. (Ephesians 1:3-5 NIV)

> There is one body and one Spirit, just as you were called to one hope when you were called; one Lord, one faith, one baptism; one God and Father of all, who is over all and through all and in all. (Ephesians 4:4-6 NIV)

The pity partier will be livid that we are pulling away from his grip. Let's ignore him and stand on God's Word. We are on the path to life! Accordingly, be sure to spend time with Jesus daily and study His Word. The Word, which is living and active, is our spiritual food and brings strength and help to us. We need it. Let's study and show ourselves approved.

Do your best to present yourself to God as one approved, a worker who does not need to be ashamed and who correctly handles the word of truth. (2 Timothy 2:15 NIV)

Our freedom is based on one thing and one thing only—the blood of Jesus Christ. He alone guarantees our salvation. If you have accepted Jesus Christ as your Savior, and you are walking in His truth as your Lord, your life will bear His fruit.

In 1899, Lewis E. Jones penned a song that is still powerful today.[10] Based on the forever truth of Revelation 7:14, here's what it says:

> Would you be free from the burden of sin?
> There's pow'r in the blood, pow'r in the blood;
> Would you o'er evil a victory win?
> There's wonderful pow'r in the blood.
>
> Would you be free from your passion and pride?
> There's pow'r in the blood, pow'r in the blood;
> Come for a cleansing to Calvary's tide;
> There's wonderful pow'r in the blood.
>
> Would you be whiter, much whiter than snow?
> There's pow'r in the blood, pow'r in the blood;
> Sin-stains are lost in its life-giving flow;
> There's wonderful pow'r in the blood.
>
> Would you do service for Jesus your King?
> There's pow'r in the blood, pow'r in the blood;
> Would you live daily His praises to sing?
> There's wonderful pow'r in the blood.

---

10. Lewis E. Jones, "Power in the Blood," 1899.

Chapter 15

Defacer of Womanhood

The saboteur hates women. Why? As a result of the fall, God placed a chasm between the serpent and the woman:

And I will put enmity between you and the woman,
and between your offspring and hers; he will crush your
head, and you will strike his heel. (Genesis 3:15 NIV)

The saboteur assaults women to bring about permanent injury and harm, and ultimately destroy them because of God's view of the woman. God specifically created the woman as a beautiful counterpart to Adam (Genesis 2:18, 21-22). Further, God determined that it would be through her body that the seed of man would pass. Life is miraculously translated into a living being within a woman's body through the marvel of gestation and birth.

God creatively arranged that a man and a woman would bring forth a human life through loving intercourse. Conceived and filled with the breath of God, children testify to the existence of God in every way. You cannot look at an infant and not see God. The truth is that each and every child is knit together and created in His image. Each might as well be tagged with a note that says: "From Elohim with great love!"

When the dragon saw that he had been hurled to the earth, he pursued the woman who had given birth to the male child. The woman was given the two wings of a great eagle, so that she might fly to the place prepared for her in the wilderness, where she would be taken care of for a time, times and half a time, out of the serpent's reach. Then from his mouth the serpent spewed water like a river, to overtake the woman and sweep her away with the torrent. But the earth helped the woman by opening its mouth and swallowing the river that the dragon had spewed out of his mouth. Then the dragon was enraged at the woman and went off to wage war against the rest of her offspring—those who keep God's commands and hold fast their testimony about Jesus. (Revelation 12:13-17 NIV)

The assault on women has landed a punch to the gut. His diabolical loathing for women has never changed. We can trace it through the biblical account and see it all around us today.

Satan is defacing women left and right, and we must speak up and help those around us.

Women are being taught to reject family. The lie penetrating the hearts of young women today is that they do not need anyone else. She does not need anyone to keep her company—no man and no child would "better" her life. What a tremendous lie this is! Like a fire on the prairie, it's been crafted by the saboteur to burn down God's desire to spread life through women.

God has another plan. Intense beauty and joy are mirrored in a marriage relationship in which a man loves his wife as Christ loves the church. These two people are not just completed by one another, but completed by the oneness found only with Christ as the Head of the union. If one is pulling hard against the other and trying to dominate them, you have an ugly marriage. We see this everywhere. These marriages don't make it because God must be the Head. Control is a vicious tool of satan that looks repugnant on anyone who is attempting to employ it over another person or a situation.

In his effort to take control himself, satan has taken a no-holds-barred approach to defacing women. Stolen purity through early violent or predatory manipulation of children, a horrific assault on our youth, has gained momentum and strength with the computer age. Additionally, gender confusion is a lie as deadly to the human heart and mind as it is to the body. Through any means necessary, the saboteur seeks vindication in the permanent scarring and defacing of woman, and the best way he can do this is through transgenderism and other queer agendas. This is true of men and women. No one is created transgender.

Through his lies and misinformation, the devil slashes the throat of the church before she can utter a word. It is time for us to wake up. Satan is defacing women left and right, and we must speak up and help those around us. We must not fall for the incendiary lies dropping like acid rain upon God's beautiful creation.

Whether you are male or female, take a moment to consider the onslaught against women in our society. Commit yourself to following God and protecting the precious lives around you in every way.

Chapter 16

Iniquitous Instigator

Have you ever heard the word *alchemy?* Not long ago, the Holy Spirit whispered this curious, almost mystical, word to my heart. Alchemy was an early form of chemistry and mystical medieval philosophy used to change (transmute) common metals into gold, finding cures for diseases, and developing potions for eternal youth.

Why should we concern ourselves with these archaic thoughts? For those who study, the answer is clear: History repeats itself. This is true with physical happenings and spiritual ones! Alchemy focused on hidden knowledge, promising eternal life and wealth through secret means. It promised the ability to create.

In his futile attempts to be like God, the saboteur has been in a frustrated and hateful state since the dawn of time. He knows the marvel of God, but swelled with his own pride in wanting to "be God," he constantly strives but can never achieve it. In the process, he has left destruction and scarring in his wake on every page of human history. There is not one page that does not bear his maniacal scratching in his loathing of God's goodness, beauty, and most of all, His creativity. We are told that early man sought the gift of fire. For satan, this is the ability to create life from nothing. That's what he wants most. And that is the specialty of God, and God alone.

Satan can never create. He can only steal materials originally created by God and use them to make false claims *ad nauseum* about himself and his Frankensteins. All he can come up with is patchwork and poor reproductions. He uses them to take us away from God.

The saboteur is always wielding a message.

He is the first one at the scene, stepping in with a bullhorn (or a whisper if that's what's called for in the moment), and ready with soulish suggestions that are pregnant with evil. (This is a good time to imagine that adder's egg hatching in one's mind.) Whatever direction he pushes, it will be counter to God's plan. He promises what he cannot give.

Just for the record, his alchemy will not produce gold, and certainly not any universal elixir you'd ever want to try. There is no "transmutation" from the saboteur's foul work to God's holy work. The gold of God's fine handiwork can never be compared to that of this unholy scientist. They have nothing whatsoever in common.

The point is to give you a picture of the saboteur's traps and devices so that when you "smell a rat," you can know without a shadow of a doubt that you have, in fact, encountered one: Beelzebub, the lord of the flies! Anything occult will exude an aroma of death. It is a sure and certain fact.

No matter what satan offers from his pharma chemistry set, we know it isn't new, and it isn't created by him. He has only combined it, not created it. He excels in taking and reshaping God's substances, which were created in wonder and for goodness, using them to bring harm and destruction on people—who are God's masterpieces!

The book of Jude has a curious statement that should be explored. When referencing the end of ungodly people, it says something quite astonishing:

> They are wild waves of the sea, foaming up their shame; wandering stars, for whom blackest darkness has been reserved forever. Enoch, the seventh from Adam, prophesied about them: "See, the Lord is coming with

thousands upon thousands of his holy ones to judge everyone, and to convict all of them of all the ungodly acts they have committed in their ungodliness, and of all the defiant words ungodly sinners have spoken against him." (Jude 13-15)

From this text, many believe that the ungodly will follow the wandering stars (fallen angels, in my opinion) to their final, non-rest-filled end. It is described as the "blackest darkness." We must not sanitize the Word and the gospel message of its real potency! In not wanting to offend, or even in a desire to be comforting, we have not been forthright on this point at times. The Word is very clear: There is no peaceful resting place for those who go on in their sin and do not acknowledge God as their Lord.

When the church could have been offering truth, it whitewashed it to appeal to more people or make it easier to tolerate.

This is why the world is throbbing with such deep wickedness and such deep despair at the same time. When the church could have been offering truth, it whitewashed it to appeal to more people or make it easier to tolerate. None of those reasons will hold up in God's court! The church has not, for the most part, told the whole truth and nothing but the truth as the Word of God tells it. Instead, we have come up with milder tones—nearly making the cross of Christ and Jesus's triumph over death and the grave of no great import.

Into the vortex of this inept, anemic, Holy Spiritless church rushed those willing to fill it with their passion for their own god. This is a very hard and very heavy word, one that is worthy of repentance for those it pricks.

In Psalm 94, there is a powerful verse, which reads, "Shall the throne of iniquity [or a corrupt throne], which devises evil by law, have fellowship with You?" (v. 20). Another version reads, "Can unjust judges be allied with You?" (CJB). The answer is clear—there can be no fellowship of God's people with those who devise evil by statute. Evil loves to set its corruption in the supposed stone of law and then point at it and say, "Now that we've accomplished *that*, who can argue with us?"

Praise God for those "but God moments" where He chooses to show mercy and compassion when we, His people, have not earned it. The truth of the matter is this: God retains the title of Judge of the earth, and there is none other who can make such a provable claim as the One who retains the authority to state it and the power to back it up! That Person is not the saboteur; it is God alone! When He moves in such a kind manner, may we—His genuine, believing, Word-delighting, Holy Spirit-listening and activated church—move in accordance with His will and not our own!

Why is this such a hugely important point? The line that comes next in Psalm 94 about those who devise evil from a place of committed iniquity is to "gather together against the life of the righteous and condemn innocent blood" (see Matthew 27:4). Such warnings about the work of the saboteur of God's people, and the work that God's people are meant to be championing in the earth, are abundantly clear. If we do not live as He called us too live, the flood of evil will overtake us. We understand this concept on so many common-sense levels, but when it comes to our spiritual health in Christ Jesus, we make so many excuses.

> Keep yourself far from a false matter; do not kill the innocent and righteous. (Exodus 23:7)

In our own mind, not involving ourselves in difficult matters somehow absolves us from the cost of the overrun of evil in our churches, our schools, our courts, our public squares, and more, but it does not. Handwringing has never been God's way. He is a Champion, a Warrior, a Defender, a Righteous Judge, and a Ruler who always gives just judgments. Never will you see God ambivalent on a matter. When you see God's people being ambivalent, it is not His way. Remember when Elijah was trying to wake up God's inheritance—His people—in Israel? He said this:

> Elijah went before the people and said, "How long will you waver between two opinions? If the LORD is God, follow him; but if Baal is God, follow him." But the people said nothing. (1 Kings 18:21 NIV)

The people saying nothing is quite a chilling moment in biblical history. However, it speaks of a right-now apathetic attitude toward God too. Elijah does eventually get a rise out of the people, but they've been in an evil stupor due to the rampant witchcraft, cavorting, manipulating, and drawing the people into deeper and deeper sin for quite some time. An awakening was vital then. And an awakening now is a must!

A stand for the intolerance of iniquity is not just a suggestion in God's mind. The saboteur in his role as instigator of iniquity will not relent. When you pull the cover off his dusty old techniques to lure you in, and you begin to take God-given steps to invite the Holy Spirit and His power into your life to combat that old serpent's ways, you will become stronger. You will be more able to recognize and resist him, and refuse his incessant invitations to party with him. It is a road to death. Do not keep calling it just "another route."

Sin is what sin is. Sin's end is what sin's end is. Shake the cobwebs of witchcraft off of the shiny advertising, and view it in its true form. Only the Holy Spirit will show you what iniquity looks like; the devil (your life-saboteur) will never do that. His mantle, his very clothing, is woven with lies. There is a reason he wears that self-developed clothing line. As long as he can keep you from viewing the wretched being that he is, he can keep leading you down to the gallows.

You, however, dear one, most beloved of the Lord, oh so fearfully and wonderfully made (Psalm 139:14), pray right now and name what has been eating at your soul, your life, and dogging your heels for far too long. Stop letting it drag you to the mortician's house! Pray this:

Dear Jesus, I call on Your strength right now. Your strength is limitless, and mine is distractable, anxious at times, and filled with all kinds of fears and doubts. Help me in my specific weaknesses (name them right now). Come near to me, God, as I confess them as sin to You. Holy Spirit, I invite You to come and lead me and guide me in Your paths, and away from the paths that have been plaguing me with wrong thinking, wrong walking, wrong talking, and wrong choice-making in my attitudes and actions. Help me to even confess them to You regularly so I might bask in Your righteousness and replace my old, worn-out, sin-stinking spiritual clothing that reeks of bad behaviors and has led me to places You never intended for me to go. You are a good God with only the best plan for my life. I love You, Lord. Amen!

Chapter 17

Mangler of Manhood

David, the epitome of genuine manhood, wrote:

Consider and hear me, O LORD my God…lest those who trouble me rejoice when I am moved. (Psalm 13:3-4)

Listen to that! The enemy wants to move you from here to there. He wants you to change your position when you are close to God, and he encourages you to take a step in the wrong direction—a step toward him. In doing this, you are choosing to move away from your God-given position *in* God. The saboteur will never motivate you to move the correct way, but if he can manipulate you to get off the spot you occupy in God, he is happy. This move comes right out of his playbook.

If you love sports, you know the importance of predicting the moves of your opponent before the next game. For us, the opposing team is that of the saboteur. He is your enemy and a very real foe. If you refuse to give up territory, you will absolutely win!

God's men need to understand this subtle tactic of the enemy. He wants to manipulate you so you relinquish your will to his, and he can move you from your sure and secure position in God to ground that is considerably more swampy. Remember, you have God's playbook! His

Word is your weapon, and God will use it to direct your heart, your thoughts, and your actions!

Jesus Himself modeled how to wield the sword against this cunning enemy (Matthew 4:1-11).

Why leave such a powerful spiritual weapon on the shelf when you have it? Why forfeit the game? Why give the enemy power over you when you do not have to? When you get a firm grip on that fact, you will be free indeed—as God's man! You, as a man, are made in the express image of God. God cannot be moved.

> He will not allow your foot to be moved; He who keeps
> you will not slumber. (Psalm 121:3)

Therefore, unless your Life-Director who loves you in truth decides to move you by His plan and will, just stay put and do what God has given you to do. We are not talking about being stubborn. This is about standing firm (Psalm 125:1).

O man of God, if you have not read Psalm 2 lately, let me encourage you to do so. Meditate on it. Allow the Holy Spirit to reign over every kingdom of your heart. Let Him into every nook and cranny, closet and drawer space, glove box, computer file and website, locker, gym bag, tool chest, and trunk space of your life. Walk Him in through prayer, and say, "Have at it all, Holy Spirit of God!" Let this be your prayer today before God, who loves you completely!

> I have set the LORD always before me; because He is at
> my right hand I shall not be moved. (Psalm 16:8)

There are places in which God has planted your feet, spiritually speaking. Through the mind of Christ, which you put on at salvation, and by the confirming work of His Holy Spirit within you, He will guide you into all truth (Philippians 2:5; John 16:13).

Then, as God's man, you shall not be moved. Period. Don't answer satan's calls. Don't listen to the devil's lies. Don't investigate his stuff through music, TV shows, movies, comics, radio, magazines, the Internet, your social media sites and apps, your friend groups, or your love interests. Make no excuses to stay in relationship with the saboteur, or with people who companion with him. Do you understand? He loathes you so much it is sickening. There is not one speck of love in him, and that's why he is yanking your chain and trying to drag you toward the pit of hell along with him. Misery loves company. Misery is the companion of fools. Read Proverbs, and study the parable of the prodigal son, paying careful attention to both brothers and their attitudes and actions.

Satan seeks to manipulate you through your soulish thoughts (mind, body, heart) in his effort to move you away from where God has placed you in His Son, Jesus Christ, through His blood.

You maintain that position by submitting your spirit man to the Holy Spirit of God. That position you get to occupy came at a great price. God sent His one and only Son that you might have that life and be able to keep that position in Christ. Jesus was not born into royalty, though He was royalty. He elected to be born into poverty in a stable. Our Savior modeled every response to sin and temptation you will ever face. He knew it all and felt it all, yet remained sinless. On the way to His death, Jesus washed people's dirty feet as a servant, even the feet of His betrayer, to model what you are to do. Then He went to a Roman cross to be crucified for you, bearing a shameful death in your place! As mentioned earlier, He literally "became sin" to redeem mankind. He won the ground on which you stand today, so don't give it up!

Man of God, hold your ground in Him. If the Father did not think Jesus's blood was enough to stay your ground in Christ, He would not have sent Him. Do not move because the enemy attempts to cheat you of your birthright and inheritance!

The new man is described this way:

> But you have not so learned Christ, if indeed you have heard Him and have been taught by Him, as the truth is in Jesus: that you put off, concerning your former conduct, the old man which grows corrupt according to

the deceitful lusts, and be renewed in the spirit of your mind, and that you put on the new man which was created according to God, in true righteousness and holiness. (Ephesians 4:20-24)

Flee also youthful lusts; but pursue righteousness, faith, love, peace with those who call on the Lord out of a pure heart. (2 Timothy 2:22)

For the grace of God that brings salvation has appeared to all men, teaching us that, denying ungodliness and worldly lusts, we should live soberly, righteously, and godly in the present age. (Titus 2:11-12)

If you are hanging around "youthful lusts" or any temptation to see what will happen, guess what? They will master you in time. You must relinquish them to Jesus. Don't be foolish enough to think you can control them on your own. Use your playbook! Hold the line!

Wisdom will save you also from the adulterous woman, from the wayward woman with her seductive words, who has left the partner of her youth and ignored the covenant she made before God. Surely her house leads down to death and her paths to the spirits of the dead. None who go to her return or attain the paths of life. (Proverbs 2:16-19 NIV)

This is a chilling passage. Pay attention, and do not be lured by this tried-and-true method of the devil. Resist him, and stay firm in your faith.

We began by describing satan as the mangler of manhood. What makes men so remarkable that satan has targeted them as he has? Why are today's festering and befouling ideologies attacking men as they are? Strong men are in the crosshairs of our cultural drive, marked for extermination. Masculinity itself has been violently attacked under the influence of the saboteur. The spirit of Jezebel (rebellion mixed with witchcraft) is the leading demonic influencer in this cacophony of loud voices.

This cry is not of human origin but carries the stench of death, hell, and the grave. In this process, human agents, being manipulated by dark spirits, are driven to destroy what they hate. These wretched and perverse spirits hate strength, responsibility, protection, provision, righteous nurture, covenant-keeping, hard work, excellent stewardship, the manly covering over the family unit, and most particularly, the love and worship of God. These are the essential, God-directed manly qualities that have been targeted for destruction. Every God-fearing man is reckoned as an enemy by demonic forces. The Jezebel spirit mows down strong men, seeking dominance. That control will belong to her and her venomous offspring—those who look and act and worship self just like she does.

Strong men are in the crosshairs of our cultural drive, marked for extermination.

With the blurring of the sexes, however, there is a new twist to the Jezebel spirit that very few could have foreseen. This spirit also elevates a twisted perversion of man. This is done through women who usurp the role of men by demonic coercion using seduction, but with the intent to control.

Jezebel raises up and nurtures "seed" on false and self-absorbed constructions. She suggests that women can be men if they "feel" like it is emerging in them. Similarly, men cavort as women if they feel like it. These putrid ideas are viper hatchlings that rise from the worship of the devil. They lead to all kinds of rampant perversity: the rape of children, even babies, as well as sex acts with animals. And worse. This is not new. It was going on in the time of Noah and will continue to the end of the age. The Bible, from the Law of Moses to the letters of Paul, addresses this kind of aberrant behavior and calls it an abomination; it is fully dis-associated from God's plan for His creation.

It would be a mistake to think these things are random. They don't just happen. They happen because people wander off the path to their own ruin.

To devolve is an idea dear to the heart of the devil. When man relinquishes his God-given position to a lesser idea of who God made him to be, perversion results. Initially, man was placed by His Creator in a garden and given a job to do. Instead, man chose to listen to the serpent, and his life was never the same again.

The Bible contains a section in which a prophecy against the human king of Babylon clearly goes to another level and describes satan's fall and doom. Isaiah 14:12 says:

> How you are fallen from heaven,
> O Lucifer, son of the morning!
> How you are cut down to the ground,
> You who weakened the nations!

If you read this chapter in its entirety, the passage shows plainly that this ugly horde, spurred on by hell's champion, goes after kings and leadership specifically. As the leaders go, so goes the nation. Similarly, the head of the home affects the entire household. Wives and children are often dragged into bad situations because of poor choices made by the one who is supposed to watch over them with care. In general, people struggle and suffer under oppressive and abusive leadership. Weakened manhood, no longer able to find its voice or God-designed qualities, walks in fear, unable to find its source in God. The saboteur knows that all it takes to destroy society is to strike the leaders.

When man concedes his role and crumples under the incessant blows leveled at him, the mangler of manhood wins. So stand firm. Stay strong. Don't move from your position in Jesus Christ that He won at the cross for You. Yes, stand up tall, O man of God! Bow your knee to God alone.

Too often, the story that fills history's pages is that man abandons his place. This is a serious issue, seen in the slow inner rot at the heart of every nation. Man is important, and the saboteur knows it. He moves in destructive ways to sabotage him, striking hard once any door is opened and any foothold given. Hell intentionally cuts off the head first—man's. Any trained warrior knows that if you can take out the leader, all you have to do is mop up the rest.

However, God's men stand and are not rendered helpless while their wives and children are harmed. They do not stand idly by. They do not join with those who seek to destroy manhood.

However, God's men stand and are not rendered helpless while their wives and children are harmed. They do not stand idly by.

Nevertheless, people are being trapped by lies that have brought down once-great civilizations. This has devastating and eternal consequences. The saboteur moves swiftly through any institution he can and sets on eradicating it entirely or attempting to twist it, thereby rendering it wholly unrecognizable.

Men matter! The enemy will target every arena of your life—your heart, your mind, your soul, your body, your spirit, and your strength. He comes to mangle your manhood, shattering every place you stand. Do not let him in when he comes knocking. Recognize him. His knocking is unrelenting because he knows you are loved devotedly by God. God sees you and designed you perfectly to deal with everything you would face. He did not expect you to go it alone, but looked forward to working with you in full cooperation with Himself. God does not leave you without His help if you will call to Him. This is true, no matter what.

God is your Helper. He had your yet unformed substance in His hands. He created you to stand and carry the office of your manhood, just as He did.

Isaiah 14 also shows how the saboteur "weakened the nations" and "ruled in anger," affording the earth no rest or quiet. It references "the sound of your stringed instruments." Lucifer is still focused on music, but his tunes, seductive and alluring to those caught in their witchcraft, are inharmonious to God's worship.

> Those who see you will gaze at you, and consider you, saying: "Is this the man who made the earth tremble, who shook kingdoms, who made the world as a wilderness and destroyed its cities, who did not open the house of his prisoners?" (Isaiah 14:16-17)

If he gets his way, this is the effect the devil can have on the leaders of the earth. Ask yourself, "Who is he to suggest anything to me?" It is Jesus's directions that matter.

Jesus proclaimed His mission when He read from the scroll of Isaiah in the synagogue. He said that this prophecy was fulfilled in Him:

> And He was handed the book of the prophet Isaiah. And when He had opened the book, He found the place where it was written: "The Spirit of the LORD is upon Me, because He has anointed Me to preach the gospel to the poor; He has sent Me to heal the brokenhearted, to proclaim liberty to the captives and recovery of sight to the blind, to set at liberty those who are oppressed; to proclaim the acceptable year of the LORD." (Luke 4:17-19)

Jesus invites all people to join Him in that mission, which is completely counter to that of the saboteur. If you compare those two passages in Isaiah, you can see that they are diametrically opposed in every possible way.

The key to the devil's appeal is his promotion of self. He recognizes that he can subtly move people away from God by pushing them to love themselves first—and without God in the picture at all, he lures them down a self-absorbed path. Many times, they don't even realize they are making the choices they are making. They never stop and think about it. The devil convinces people that their way is a good one, all ways work, and that they are safe. He will do anything and say anything to keep people from a relationship with Jesus—the One who *keeps* His promises.

> A man who has friends must himself be friendly, but there
> is a friend who sticks closer than a brother. (Proverbs 18:24)

This describes Jesus perfectly. He is an eternal Friend who will not abandon you at any time. Jesus counted the cost and obediently did what His Father sent Him to do. Only Jesus wears the victor's crown. He alone bears the scars to prove how He sticks by you, doing more than most brothers would ever do (John 15:13). He took your shame, your guilt, and your sin to the cross, and then it was buried with Him. Unlike any other, He rose up, taking His life up again in the triumph of His resurrection. To believe in Jesus is to be part of His family, restored to continue His work. He will never leave you or lie to you (Numbers 23:19).

Satan has not accomplished anything for you. Instead, he makes claims and wants to strike deals that he hopes you cannot resist. He lies all the time, and he's predatory, capable of shapeshifting so he can confuse and use you for his own selfish ends. The saboteur appeals unremittingly to your flesh. The only way to counteract his onslaughts is to surrender your spirit to God, and put on God's armor every day (Ephesians 6:10-19).

When you invite Jesus in as your Savior and exalt Him as your Lord, He will be! He delights in helping you. He will faithfully help you lead as you were designed to do. This leadership will bear the insignia of the Holy Spirit as He flows through you and you abide in Him (John 15:4).

There are three areas the devil assaults heavily; they are compromise, exchange, and negotiation. Adam was in a lovingly designed garden with everything he needed—communion with God, a helpmate, and plenty else. What is the mangler of manhood's first scheme? He intercepted Adam through compromise.

By suggesting that he had not been given enough by God, Adam became dissatisfied. The enemy further urged Adam to reach for something beyond it—something more, something hidden. He was questioning God's trustworthiness, as though God were holding back this great and mysterious wealth. Man made the first exchange. He exchanged what he had (which was very good) for an unknown (which was very bad). The saboteur (disguised as the serpent) made the fruit seem like more than it was. He is exceptionally good at verbal marketing. Truth, however, is nowhere present in any of his exchanges.

Some think that it was unkind of God to put Adam and Eve in such a position. God was very clear though. He made plain what the cost to Adam would be, so he knew. The saboteur, promoting himself through the cunning serpent, gained the ear (and eventually, the trust) of Adam and Eve. Appealing to their sight as well, he pulled off the hoax of the age because they listened to him. You see, they had eaten the fruit in their heart before it ever entered their body. This continues today.

Through lust over what we do not possess, the enemy convinces people to believe lies to get what they want.

How did the saboteur achieve such a feat? How did he lure man into giving up His birthright for such a poor pot of porridge? Through negotiation, that's how.

He used strong visual manipulation, highlighting the one thing in all of God's magnificent creation that he knew man was instructed not to take. He mystified it and deified it, elevating the desire for it above God. He could not pluck that fruit for them, so he convinced them to take it. He moved God's creation into a dangerous place while making it seem like it was the deal of a lifetime!

Through lust over what we do not possess, the enemy convinces people to believe lies to get what they want. He does this all the time. Through temptation, he decouples you from trusting in God, making you believe you can have things God does not want for you.

Temptations are present in every man's life. What is the devil working on you about? When you identify it, you will be able to see his methods, and Jesus can help you with it. Add it to your knowledge of his playbook.

Standing far away in time, you wonder, What did Adam think was going to happen?

As a bystander, affected by original sin, from this opening act of diabolical outrage, you stand wondering, *How could Adam not know what the cost was going to be?* You stand back, looking through corrupted lenses, in full wonderment. Why did he give up something so valuable—his life, his work, his family, and all that would follow?

Adam's decision over that one thing would spill death over it all!

How could a piece of fruit signal death? That fruit represented a compromise of the love of God and the trust they shared before that moment. It represented the union and intimacy they had with a Creator who had shown them camaraderie, fellowship, and abundant provision while withholding absolutely nothing. Adam and Eve lacked nothing. Not one thing. They just did not know that.

The negotiation required to move mankind away from their intimate position with God happened with the addition of one impure thought. Like a single drop of ink diffuses and colors a beaker of water, so began the domino effect.

Though Adam had no cause to think the serpent as anything unusual, the introduction of an impure thought began its diabolical work—the breakdown of man's trust in the goodness of God. One impure thought is all it took. That's how the devil stole what was not his.

The mangler couldn't wait to destroy Adam. He hated that beautiful garden, full of God's goodness humming all about him in its epic and astounding glory. He craved man's position. He could not let man stand there, holding the authority of God, when he didn't even know what it was. God loved man, so the devil hated them. He still does.

Cunning is not wisdom, not even a form of it. It is an evil tool of manipulation, born in a heart that envies what another possesses. Many cultures celebrate cunning and call it wisdom. Cunning is wrapped in deception, so it is not of God, but is earthly, compromised, and impure. God's wisdom is higher, and it's the wisdom you need. Pray this prayer of restoration:

Jesus, You are the Head. You are my Master. I am Your servant, first and foremost, above all my other roles as a man. As You lead me, I am enabled to lead, help, and serve others in a fashion worthy of Your character. As You lead, I am able to conduct myself with right heart attitudes. Through time with You in prayer and in Your Word, as well as in fellowship with other believers, I choose to prioritize Your ways. I can only be truly successful by listening and obeying Your voice within me. I will uphold Your standards, stated in Your Word, which I understand are counter to the world's. My body is Your temple, so I will allow nothing unclean within it.

When I fail, help me to repent and set my way straight in You again. Jesus, You made me a man because You considered me worthy for that role. You intended me to look to the Holy Spirit to teach me wisdom and guide me in all my ways so I might think right, act right, and lead in love, shouldering the responsibilities of the role You gave me as a man. Thank You for leading me well so I may lead others and touch lives for You. Restore and remake me into the man You want me to be. I trust You, Father God, knowing You to be good. I will fear You above all and set You before me continually, my loving Savior, King Jesus! Amen.

Chapter 18

Furtive Faith-Fracturer

The saboteur does not have to turn us completely in the opposite direction in life; he only needs to mathematically and strategically adjust our trajectory, which will automatically alter our destination coordinates.

He does this by redirecting our trust, even in miniscule ways. There are a lot of "good people" (far too many) who are off course and do not know it. The saboteur's intention is to cripple our faith and deter the plan of God for our life.

What does this well-loved verse in Romans 8 tell us?

> Yet in all these things we are more than conquerors through Him who loved us. For I am persuaded that neither death nor life, nor angels nor principalities nor powers, nor things present nor things to come, nor height nor depth, nor any other created thing, shall be able to separate us from the love of God which is in Christ Jesus our Lord. (Romans 8:37-39)

That sounds thorough, doesn't it? Why then do so many Christians operate as "less than" conquerors and behave as though their lives are awful, evidenced by the fact that their mouth is filled with an unending stream of complaints?

Could this problem be related to our continual decision to listen to the enemy's endless dripping of all things evil? Yes, it can. He spills these into our ear and eye gates, and we entertain them by our own free will and through our interaction with it. Garbage in, garbage out. It is interesting that this verse, which so magnificently champions the love of God, also mentions angels, principalities, and powers. How much understanding do we have in this area?

Are we aware that rebellious angels, demonic forces, wicked principalities, and powers are actively at work in the world around us to unseat our faith in Jesus Christ and our belief in God? Does that seem ludicrous? I assure you, it is not. We know that because the Writer of the Word, God Himself, lovingly chose to inform us that these evils exist. He conquered them through His Christ, the Messiah, Jesus! Therefore, we must be on actual guard against their infiltration. Jesus conquered death, hell, and the grave, and because we, as believers, live *in and through* Jesus, we are conquerors too.

Let me help you with this concept. In this chapter, we will look at the faith-fracturer!

Imagine your doorbell rings, and on your doorstep, there is a package from King Jesus Himself. Redemption and salvation are in the package. It is the best gift you will ever open! You can't even compare it to a Christmas present, as all Christmas offerings pale miserably by comparison.

The package is marked by the Sender. The Bible says He died "once and for all" (Romans 6:10). No claimants to the gift can say He was not equitable and thorough in His work! In His own words, "It is finished!" As we look at it, we are immediately struck by the fact that God took the trouble to put this together and send it to us. We are in awe of the package itself.

Jesus died to save our eternal soul. He understood that we could not redeem ourselves. We were sentenced to death and separation from God because of our sin, but God wanted us anyway. He had a plan that would provide redemption for those who wanted to be with Him. It was a costly venture, but God went through with it.

He loved us so passionately that He took our place. He came down, clothed Himself with human flesh, lived a sinless life, and then took the blame and bore the shame and the scourge of sin. He endured terrible pain, bearing what you and I could never have borne. And He did it for everyone! He followed the Father's clear redemption plan. Jesus, the only begotten Son, carried out that difficult obedience to the absolute letter of the Mosaic Law—meeting its every requirement. And He did it for us.

Considering the difficulty of the task, we should be grabbing the box and running indoors to open it and explore more about Jesus and His kingdom. All too often though, we make a confession of faith in Jesus, and think, *Well, I did it.* Then we leave the package and its incredible contents out on the porch under the rocker. In doing this, we never fully discover, test, or appreciate the salvation Jesus offers us in its fullness. We miss the main point of our salvation entirely. We willfully miss the fullness of Jesus's love and plan for our life, and will not grow in knowing Him. In this way, the faith-fracturer has redirected us from our initial calling.

John pens it best in Jesus's warning to the church in Ephesus:

> Nevertheless I have this against you, that you have left
> your first love. (Revelation 2:4)

I don't know about you, but if Jesus wrote that about me, I would be utterly devastated. Many believers today, and throughout history, regarded their faith with an apathetic yawn, so they looked like this to Jesus. They had lost their first love—Him. Does this sound like a bride ready to walk down the aisle to meet her Beloved? Definitely not.

We must pay attention to this. God considers us His dear ones. He calls us His beloved because that is how He feels about us. He died for us, rose again, and then sent His Holy Spirit to teach us truth and godly wisdom so He could lead us in power, giving us the ability to help others as well as ourselves. What more do we need to see from Him? What more could He possibly give?

> Multitudes, multitudes in the valley of decision! For the day
> of the LORD is near in the valley of decision. (Joel 3:14)

Is this you? Have you had your faith hijacked by indifference brought on by the saboteur after your initial confession of faith? Did the birds (the enemy) swoop down and repurpose your life to fit his pride-filled desire for you instead of God's? Pray about this right now. Ask the Holy Spirit if you need to repent because you have treated the gift of salvation indifferently. If you have, tell God you are sorry and mean it. Stay with Him, and let Him minister to your heart. Then, begin to walk obediently before it is too late. We have one precious life. We must use it well and for God's glory, not our own, and definitely not in accordance with evil.

The saboteur relentlessly whispers doubt into our soul, hoping to conquer our spirit.

Back to that package! Let's get it off the doorstep, bring it into the house, and open it! God's love naturally encourages movement on our part. But perhaps we are feeling kind of bad that we had to repent. We have not followed Him as we ought. Condemnation is a favorite pastime in the mouth of the saboteur. He will use any means possible to keep you down. Thank You, Jesus, for Your mercy.

> Who is he who condemns? It is Christ who died, and
> furthermore is also risen, who is even at the right hand of
> God, who also makes intercession for us. (Romans 8:34)

Nevertheless, the saboteur relentlessly whispers doubt into our soul, hoping to conquer our spirit. We must rebuke him and deny him access. Jesus conquered. He is all-powerful. His work is completely intact, fixed, and immoveable—a Rock to stand on! So stand on Christ and do not choose another way; one way leads to misery and failure while the other leads to peace and life.

Unbelief is a particularly slippery slope. Jesus spoke about this a lot, and powerfully! Here's just one instance:

> "You unbelieving and perverse generation," Jesus replied, "how long shall I stay with you? How long shall I put up with you? Bring the boy here to me." (Matthew 17:17 NIV)

Why did Jesus call them unbelieving and perverse? These may seem like odd word choices for Jesus, but that is how He viewed their lack of faith and self-absorption. They were so consumed with themselves that they didn't possess enough faith to allow His healing and restoration to flow through them to another hurting human being!

Sometimes the shock of Jesus's words jar us enough to recognize that the path we are on is *not* the path of life after all. In His eyes, we are in a totally different place altogether, and when we take the time to think about what He says, we wake up. Thank You, Jesus! His perspective is the only vantage point that matters. God's opinion should inform us on how we are doing.

Too many people today allow the world to inform their faith when it should be the reverse of that. Our faith in God should be informing the world. When did this fatal mix-up happen? It was when we allowed the faith-fracturer to rewrite the script that Jesus wrote about our faith.

Let's get back to Matthew 17 though: The boy had a demon—one that had been tossing him around for years as though he were a dog's toy. According to the child's father, it had continuously tried to kill him throughout his young life.

> He has seizures and is suffering greatly. He often falls into the fire or into the water. I brought him to your disciples, but they could not heal him. (Matthew 17:15-16 NIV)

Jesus's followers came up short in this situation, but Jesus did not. He healed the child, and all who were in attendance were humbled. Thank God for His mercy.

Let's get this straight once and for all: satan is not the author of faith; satan is the author of faithlessness.

So why do so many Christians follow cosplaying, faithless hirelings instead of true undershepherds of the faith? Why are so many of us open to the world's influencers, entertainers, professors, family, and friends—those who do not confess Jesus as Lord—to inform our faith in God? Why should we look to them at all?

Why ask a murderer and liar what he thinks about the Master of the Universe? While the saboteur would love to lay claim to that title, he never will.

Unbelief is a silent foe—one of which we are often unaware.

Unbelief is a silent foe—one of which we are often unaware. In this account in Matthew, those trying to cast out that demon were unaware of their unbelief. They didn't see it standing in the way of their faith. This can happen to us too, so let's take a minute and ask Jesus about this right now. Pray this prayer before we go on:

> *Lord, I know unbelief is not of You. If it exists in me, root it out right now in Your powerful name. If this needs to be a daily prayer for a while, so be it. Please guide me in this, Holy Spirit. Thank You, Lord!*

Let Jesus, the trustworthy One, go through your closet and toss out the wretched, earthly garments that don't suit you any longer as a child of light. This is part of our salvation package! We are children of light. Let Him be thorough! Rest in this sacred time with Jesus. Let Him influence your heart, your thoughts, and your speech. May He cleanse us fully. Ask Him for growth in self-control too. No one likes to find that they've arrived at the wrong town when they thought they were on the road to another destination entirely. Spending time like this with Jesus prevents that kind of blindsiding. It stops the devil's plan, laying waste to the layers of sabotage he has placed around us.

Let's look at another portion of Scripture that exposes multiple tactics of the devil in just a few lines:

> An ungodly man digs up evil,
> And it is on his lips like a burning fire.
> A perverse man sows strife,
> And a whisperer separates the best of friends.
> A violent man entices his neighbor,
> And leads him in a way that is not good.
> He winks his eye to devise perverse things;
> He purses his lips and brings about evil.

Proverbs 16:27-30

Here we find two very useful and highly effective stratagems. Let's uncover them right now. Remember, the enemy is not inventive, but he is tactical. That's right, tactical. He is strategic. Other words for a *stratagem* are scheme or plot. We would like to avoid these. Every move he makes is tactical and planned to achieve his desired end, whether it is a large battle or just a skirmish.

As the true Hero and Savior of the world, the Maker of the heavens and earth, the only wise God, Jesus discloses and unmasks the debauched and defiled, twisted and obscured methods the saboteur utilizes in our life. When we see them for ourselves, we can pray them out of our life, and then out of the lives of those in our family, including our friends and any who come to know the Lord.

There are two tactical devices the Holy Spirit wants to expose in this chapter. They are the power of the drift and the wearing down of the saints.

When we were children, my father and mother took us on many vacations to pretty, restful places for a week or two at a time. During these times, chunks of our daylight hours were used by my father to write his many books. Each outlined a particular revelation the Holy Spirit had given him. They had many themes: politics, the church, the direction of the present world government, our national government, economics, God's holiness, the baptism of the Holy Spirit, his own testimony, along with a biographical work highlighting the miracles God had done to get him where he was at that time.

My dad scratched feverishly as the Lord poured it out through him onto legal-sized yellow memo pads. I remember pages and pages on the millennium, a largely untouched subject at that time. The millennium refers to a time when God's saints will rule and reign with Him within a totally righteous government administered completely and gloriously by Him, allowing us to work alongside Him. What a marvelous promise!

Getting back to the subject at hand, it was during these fruitful and adventurous journeys that my father wrote a hugely popular book on the work of the enemy. Again, not much had been written on the subject at that time, and people were hungry for understanding. They had questions and needed answers. Incidentally, the church at that time was also undereducated on this topic and mired in the tactics of the enemy, all while on the cusp of a complete change.

Understanding sent them careening headlong into transformation under the capable hand of Almighty God as He taught us everything Jesus, the Son, had to say! Today, nearly fifty years later, the church is still in the same place. Many are largely ignorant of satanic devices, so the Holy Spirit is pressing firmly on this next generation to learn and awaken.

God's love is far too great—too awesome and too kind—to leave us floundering in our unbelief, powerlessness, and blindness. He knows that the fire in our heart must be rekindled to meet the critical demands of our culture. Many still do not know Him at all.

> For the Spirit God gave us does not make us timid, but gives
> us power, love and self-discipline. (2 Timothy 1:7 NIV)

All that has been said here is true, but even though correction and transformation must occur, it happens out of unspeakable love. Yes, the authentic church of Jesus has many outstanding qualities. We have God's Son living in us. He is the Savior, or Bishop, of our soul. He will not leave us in our present condition of unbelief, blindness, and powerlessness. He is with us to recognize when unbelief is present—in our heart, our family, and so on.

> **We, His bride, are set on biting and devouring one another—the same problem the disciples and apostles dealt with in the early church.**

Once we identify how much and how far and how deeply we have been used like dog toys, we can seek God. Look for the areas in which you gnaw on one another or are redirected through the sickening, easy-grab demonic tincture of offense. We can meet Him at the altar, confessing our sorrow over this. He will help us. But we need to take a serious look: We, His bride, are set on biting and devouring one another—the same problem the disciples and apostles dealt with in the early church. It is still happening today. Religion and a religious spirit are never of God, but they are chief tactics of the devil.

Get rid of offense, and get rid of that religious spirit; it was odious to God in Jesus's ministry days, and it still is in ours! We have not progressed; we have regressed. We have not evolved; we have devolved. We look more like the saboteur, while calling our process "transformation"! Jesus, the Bishop of our soul, and the Holy Spirit, should shine in us like an ornament reflecting a life that is submitted to God.

The witness of Stephen, the first martyr in the early church, and his shining face comes to mind. When Moses spent time in the presence of God, he emerged with a shining face. It was so obvious that the onlookers could not deny God's presence there. We too must seek this place, even though we are not always cognizant of it in ourselves. This is the kind of true transformative work that the Lord wants to see—the kind made possible by the Holy Spirit's power.

Any manner in which we try to make this happen on our own is not acceptable. Some churches suggest we self-manifest, which is an ugly, demonic phrase. We bring offerings to God like Abel did. We want to be like Abraham, Elijah, Paul, Esther, Mary, Stephen, and so many others. His powerful, holy, living Word chronicles them all. They model an offering of the self to the Holy Spirit so He can transform it in a real, deep, and lasting way. As the Holy Spirit guides, our soul finds rest in Him and doesn't try to take the lead. We don't want our families and churches driven by the saboteur and his agents of subterfuge!

As the Holy Spirit guides, our soul finds rest in Him and doesn't try to take the lead.

This subject continually goes back to prayer. As we seek God to root unbelief out of us, He wants us to stand firm and continue in prayer until we see change. There is hope. If there was not, this book would not have been written. Instead, it was birthed in my spirit by the Holy Spirit and poured out onto these pages like molten-hot lava flowing over the landscape of my own soul first! Take a stand! Intercede for yourself, and then others, as the Holy Spirit directs you. Prayer is the dynamo of Holy Spirit revelation, which explains why prayer has been hijacked and assaulted by the saboteur in many churches and Christian gatherings.

The enemy of our soul has always known that if we pray as we ought, nothing will stop the bride of Christ, His church, from unseating wicked schemes in the church and in the world. Meanwhile, unbelievers are but sheep being slaughtered daily.

> You have planted them, yes, they have taken root;
> They grow, yes, they bear fruit.
> You are near in their mouth

> But far from their mind.
>
> But You, O LORD, know me;
> You have seen me,
> And You have tested my heart toward You.
> Pull them out like sheep for the slaughter,
> And prepare them for the day of slaughter.
> How long will the land mourn,
> And the herbs of every field wither?
> The beasts and birds are consumed,
> For the wickedness of those who dwell there,
> Because they said, "He will not see our final end."
>
> Jeremiah 12:2-4

Think on the words above: "You are near in their mouth but far from their mind" (literally, their most secret parts). They were not set on God in their heart, and Jesus simply will not accept an unprepared bride, nor should we expect Him to do so! He is our Bishop! We need to throw out the religious connotations and equally religious garb that come to mind when we think of the word *bishop*.[11]

As it refers to Jesus, *bishop* is the One who is the ultimate Overseer of all that happens in the flock of the Lord Jesus Christ! The flock does not belong to the pastors. They are undershepherds, like tenant farmers tending to that which is not theirs. Jesus is the Shepherd. We belong to Him alone—a spiritual fact He made very clear. Those pastors who understand this are servants of the Most High and care for His flock. Then there are those who steal the title of "bishop of souls," seeing them-selves as overseers and owners of "their" flock. They build their own kingdom, and not God's. If you are a pastor, pray and ask the Holy Spirit for His opinion on how you are caring for His people—and then pray some more, beloved!

---

11. Please pick up my precious friend's book, *Splendid Day*, by Mary Soler on this topic, it is a must-read.

Prayer is where we remain, not a place we get up from. We are often too quick to "get up" from our prayer time. We can't just "pray our way to health" as a church! The multiple times this has been said by the mouths of powerful Christians over the past few years has been appalling. Though it would be my preference to tell you this attitude does not exist, it does. This should never be said. Never! In their defense, many who are actively fighting hard battles, are actually angry with Christians who "stay by the saddlebags" (Judges 5:15-17; 1 Samuel 10:21-22) and just say they'll pray. These believers know nothing about battle strategy and simply lift uncarbonated prayers listlessly into the air. That's a sad trade-off for the fine, deadly, and accurately targeted arrows they could have if they were directed by the Holy Spirit in prayer. God's will hits its intended target in the saboteur's camp (not people).

The Power of the Drift

> We must pay the most careful attention, therefore, to what we have heard, so that we do not drift away. For since the message spoken through angels was binding, and every violation and disobedience received its just punishment, how shall we escape if we ignore so great a salvation? This salvation, which was first announced by the Lord, was confirmed to us by those who heard him. God also testified to it by signs, wonders and various miracles, and by gifts of the Holy Spirit distributed according to his will. (Hebrews 2:1-4 NIV)

On one of our vacations when I was a child, we traveled as a family to the beach. Looking back, I see an unusual, carefree fearlessness that hovered around my life. Today, I can attribute this to the years when my parents were steeped in evangelizing the gospel message, which included water baptism and the mighty work of the baptism of the Holy Spirit.

On this particular occasion, and for a few, short days, playing in the ocean waves was my daily, sunburnt but happy ritual! I spent hours in the ocean. However, one day, I was suddenly overwhelmed with panic when I realized I'd lost a fix on my parents' umbrella. That might not seem chilling to you, but it was for me at the time.

I'd like to use this picture as an analogy for the continual attack of the faith-fracturer! Remember, I'd been in the ocean for hours, and even though my swimming capability was fairly keen, the next several minutes were terrifying.

I'd been happily drifting along for some time—watching clouds, listening to seabirds scream as they wheeled above me, hearing the happy laughter and welcome murmur of voices from the shore, even seeing a rainbow or two. I'd been carried out quite a distance from the shoreline and had now drifted down quite a ways so that when I looked, I did not recognize even one distinguishing feature on the beach. And I definitely could not see my parents' umbrella!

An explosion of fear enveloped me. I had never felt such fear before. I paddled frantically to return to shore again, even if I could not recognize which section I was in—but I only drifted further out. Now terror heightened my already fearful heart!

I was not making any headway even though I was swimming steadily. I didn't know it, but I was fighting against a riptide, which is a very strong current. The more I labored to go forward to the shore, the more I was carried "down beach." Anyone who has experienced this firsthand knows it is not fun and can prove deadly. Basically, you weary yourself; you can make no forward progress to reach the shore until you are out of the current that is stopping you.

After a while, I did make it to shore. Then I walked toward the only recognizable tall structure I knew until I spotted my family. From that time on, the ocean took on another cast. My respect for it grew. Though friendly, it had its dangers.

What analogy can be seen here? The faith-fracturer chisels away frantically at us, though he's often undetected by our spiritual senses. As a result, we underestimate the drift that may be going on in our spiritual life. Should we leave it alone—untended and neglected—he will take us far out to sea with the intent to drown us, or at the very least, keep us from shore so we can't get regrounded again! We must always be intentionally on guard and sober of our faith.

The sad truth is that drifting is easy. We just float along, letting all the flotsam and jetsam of the world flow over us. What could be the harm?

The Bible teaches us to not casually accept other doctrines, beliefs, or ideologies—new or old. If anything does not line up with our Bible-grounded faith, we must resist it. The prophets of old, as well as the apostles, disciples, and righteous saints before us warned continuously of such faulty thinking. It is in this vulnerable condition, when you are not even aware that anything serious is happening, that your now-flailing faith can be crushed. The saboteur has been waiting for just such a faith-lulling, dulling moment to take us out.

The faith-fracturer chisels away frantically at us, though he's often undetected by our spiritual senses.

Our faith, grounded in belief, is a garden to be tended regularly. It is a home to be locked at night and watched over during the day. Our faith is the bedrock of all that is built on top of it, but it will not sustain the work of two builders. Only one. His name is Jesus, the Lord of your life. If you accept another architect and builder, your faith is not in Him anymore. Pluralism will not be tolerated by our Savior. There is no room for it.

When we even think we can serve more than one master, that is a sign that we are already far adrift from the shore. In some manner, these thoughts have penetrated the inner walls of our faith. When this happens, we need to pray and ask the Holy Spirit, "Have I become adrift in an ocean of other beliefs? Have I become stuck in the strong riptide of unbelief?" If He says yes, ask Him for help. He will come!

In whatever way we drift, Jesus will always help us find our way back to shore when we cry out to Him. He will help us get regrounded in Him, and none other. If you sinned during this time in some specific way, name it, repent, and ask for God's help with it. If you invited another "god" into your life, ask the Holy Spirit to help you name it as the Bible does, and repent. Come back to the shore of faith in Jesus. Fear and panic will not help you, but the Holy Spirit of God will! In Jesus's name, renounce all invitations to demon spirits. Re-invite the Holy Spirit to take up residence once more after thoroughly cleansing your spiritual home.

Remember, if you have invited or allowed other spirits in, there will be a fight to keep you from allowing Jesus back into those areas, and that antagonism may surface in multiple areas. This is a sure indicator that there has been a drift, so don't let it deter you from doing the necessary work right now to get back to shore. Do not put it off until tomorrow. Once the saboteur is in the door, he is loath to lose a victim, particularly one who was in the faith. He loves to tempt a Christian away from their faith in Jesus. Don't imagine that this cannot happen. It can, so be warned and be careful.

The Wearing Down of the Saints

The faith-fracturer has a secondary, and just as deadly, tactic, which is the wearying of the saints. The goal of this scheme is to get a believer so obliterated by the many-pronged and unrelenting attack on their faith that they simply drop from exhaustion—so battered and bruised that they are wholly unfit for battle. If this is you, you must invite the body of Christ to join you in prayer for help! Everyone who is a mature saint of the Lord Jesus Christ will have at least one such moment like this in their life. Some may even experience a season like this.

This experience is dangerous for your faith life because it is here that the saboteur deals his "death blows." He has, through the careful placing of stratagems, intentionally brought you to his slaughterhouse of faith. Many a precious warrior, a good warrior, a knowledgeable warrior, has dropped on this field!

In this restless, wearied place, we are desperate for rejuvenation, restoration, and peace. The saboteur rolls by just then with his wicked cart of wares. His cart is full: sexual sin and perversion, substance abuse and addictions, greed, envy, and covetousness appear with a myriad of ways to get around God's laws. On top of that, as you thumb through the saboteur's faith-fracturer subscriptions, you will find the enticing ones highlighted just for you.

> For all that is in the world—the lust of the flesh, the lust
> of the eyes, and the pride of life—is not of the Father but
> is of the world. (1 John 2:16)

When you are wearied to the bone—physically and emotionally—because you have been battered and buffeted by the very real assignations of the enemy, he then rides in like a savior or a hero. His "help" may come in the form of a potion or a relationship you think you need. He appears as an angel of light. Now who wouldn't want to see an angel—or just a little light when you're that exhausted, right? Wrong!

> And no wonder! For Satan himself transforms himself
> into an angel of light. (2 Corinthians 11:14)

But we have other options, don't we? We are part of a family of Bible-believing, praying saints who will lift us up and lay hands on us. We must take care to go to no other source to unweary ourselves. We must stick with God's people! I didn't say religious people, but God's people. Find the ones who truly know God, and ask them to pray for you from His Word. When you pray, ask that your faith may be refreshed, that you might have strength in your fight, and the understanding that you are not battling your circumstances alone. Do not, as the saboteur will suggest to you, think it is embarrassing to ask for prayer and support in your present, wearied status. That is exactly what we are supposed to do!

> From the end of the earth I will cry to You, when my
> heart is overwhelmed; lead me to the rock that is higher
> than I. (Psalm 61:2)

Your advice comes from the Word, your power comes from the Word, your prayer instruction comes from the Word, your ability to stand in any debilitating storm is the body of Christ's mandate. Prayer is powerful, but if you keep your situation hidden from the body of Christ, you are placing yourself in spiritual danger. Moses needed Aaron and Hur to hold up his arms in battle, and so do you. Go get prayer!

Chapter 19

Disgusting Demoralizer

Hezekiah, king of Judah, and his people were being besieged in every way. The name Hezekiah means "Jehovah is my strength." The enemy pressed his propaganda hard upon the king and God's people so they would give up, weakening them. This is the result of heeding the enemy's lies and plans.

> Then the Rabshakeh said to them, "Say now to Hezekiah, 'Thus says the great king, the king of Assyria: "What confidence is this in which you trust? You speak of having plans and power for war; but they are mere words. And in whom do you trust, that you rebel against me? Now look! You are trusting in the staff of this broken reed, Egypt, on which if a man leans, it will go into his hand and pierce it. So is Pharaoh king of Egypt to all who trust in him. But if you say to me, 'We trust in the LORD our God,' is it not He whose high places and whose altars Hezekiah has taken away, and said to Judah and Jerusalem, 'You shall worship before this altar in Jerusalem'?"'" (2 Kings 18:19-22)

This was the taunt of the enemy forces against them: Just give up! There's no way out! But God said differently:

I will lead the blind by ways they have not known,
along unfamiliar paths I will guide them; I will turn
the darkness into light before them and make the rough
places smooth. These are the things I will do; I will not
forsake them. (Isaiah 42:16 NIV)

"Be strong and courageous; do not be afraid nor dismayed
before the king of Assyria, nor before all the multitude
that is with him; for there are more with us than with
him. With him is an arm of flesh; but with us is the LORD
our God, to help us and to fight our battles." And the
people were strengthened by the words of Hezekiah king
of Judah. (2 Chronicles 32:7-8)

Everything about Hezekiah's situation was dire! There was no "escape pod" like in the movies. There was no hero. Even Sennacherib's general truthfully named all the cities they'd taken and gutted before arriving in Jerusalem.

This is exactly how his demoralization works today too. If you do not recognize him, you'll fall into the same booby trap as previous generations under his skilled, evil plans. Remember, though he is not creative, he is cunning. Never underestimate him. He wants your head on a platter too!

Go to God and tell Him what's happening. That's exactly what Hezekiah did. He prostrated himself before God in the temple, asking for help, and God sent it.

In the book of Nehemiah, the devil does the same thing. He comes to ridicule, insult, and stir up frustrations, so you will act out. He wants to discourage God's people.

And in the presence of his associates and the army of
Samaria, he said, "What are those feeble Jews doing?
Will they restore their wall? Will they offer sacrifices?
Will they finish in a day? Can they bring the stones back
to life from those heaps of rubble—burned as they are?"
Tobiah the Ammonite, who was at his side, said, "What

they are building—even a fox climbing up on it would break down their wall of stones!" Hear us, our God, for we are despised. Turn their insults back on their own heads. Give them over as plunder in a land of captivity." (Nehemiah 4:2-4 NIV)

The very reason the accusers came to discourage Nehemiah's work was not because they were not making progress, but because they were. In fact, they were making swift work in exactly the right direction. Their success caused panic and fear in the heart of their enemy. Their criminal plan was about to be shifted in a big way!

The minute we think we can do better than God is the moment the disgusting demoralizer finds a foothold.

Psalm 109:1-5 (NIV) reflects the pain a believer feels when attacked for doing the right thing.

> My God, whom I praise,
> do not remain silent,
> for people who are wicked and deceitful
> have opened their mouths against me;
> they have spoken against me with lying tongues.
> With words of hatred they surround me;
> they attack me without cause.
> In return for my friendship they accuse me,
> but I am a man of prayer.
> They repay me evil for good,
> and hatred for my friendship.

Invite God's plan to supersede all others, and let the Holy Spirit "de-spirit" the demonic spirits at work to bring you harm!

Moses did this. Esther did this. Daniel did this. Paul did this. Peter did this. Mary did this. Hannah did this. David did this.

God moves when we *trust* Him, believing He is good and knows what is best for our life. The minute we think we can do better than God is the moment the disgusting demoralizer finds a foothold. He intends to lock you in his jail cell of anxiety and depression, shackling you in darkness and chains. In that darkness, he speaks lie after lie in an effort to put his foot on your neck in victory.

Call on God and tell Him you need Him. Repent for thinking you didn't need Him and for trying to arrange things according to your own plan. God will answer a sincere cry, made in humility of heart, mind, and soul. He will build up your strength to combat the enemy. God will always pick up the phone. He doesn't let it go to His answering machine; He doesn't own one! God is available 24/7!

Chapter 20

Puppet Master

Those involved with witchcraft are puppets being manipulated by a dark master who never tells his "worshippers" the truth. In fact, a lying spirit goes hand in hand in this.

I recently saw a hideous display on social media that illustrates this. It was a post of a lovely young girl under this influence. A Svengali of human souls had completely absorbed this girl's every movement, using her arms like two serpents mating, while her eyes stared wide, dead, and fixated, as though she were in a drugged trance. A seductive spirit leered from her eye sockets. She seemed fully darkened within as though all her God-given sensibilities had been removed and she was completely submitted to the saboteur's agenda instead. He had total control.

Sorrow and grief flooded my heart, and prayer flowed out of my mouth. It was heartbreaking to see someone being so terribly used by the evil one! She called herself a dancer but showed no emotion whatsoever. A mesmerizing spirit of witchcraft controlled her body, and even though the lights weren't on behind her eyes, someone was home—and it wasn't the girl! Demons controlled her every move.

Unfortunately, since people in the church are uncomfortable about dealing with this sort of thing, it has reached epidemic levels. Jesus is in the business of setting people free—not making them cushy in their pews. It is way past time to deal with this, so at the risk of offending a few people and stepping on religious toes, let's get on with it!

We sometimes hear of familiar spirits. They show up as "friendly" and can look like your grandparent or a lost child.

Its very name, witchcraft, is illuminating, but before we dig into that, please pray as follows:

> *Lord Jesus, I ask by the power of the living Christ that You will reveal to me what I need to know this instant. I pray You will bind up, even now, the strong man (any demonic forces) and any person or hindrance of my flesh. Jesus, let me hear what Your Holy Spirit would say to me. Keep my mind clear and my heart open to hear what is about to be delivered to me as truth from God's holy Word and God's Holy Spirit, which can only speak truth to me. I declare that the Holy Spirit of Jesus Christ is God and none other. Let me hear only His voice, so I silence, in Jesus's strong and powerful name, all other voices from speaking to me right now. Jesus, I loose Your power to deliver me from whatever has kept me bound, whatever has kept me from hearing, whatever has kept me from obeying, and whatever has hidden the truth from illuminating my soul by the power of God almighty and His precious Holy Spirit, who was given to me for this purpose. I declare right now that Jesus Christ alone is Lord.*

If you cannot say those last five italicized words, you may be dealing with a demonic spirit from which you need to be set free. Demons cannot say those words. They do not want you free either. They like having a free ride inside your life—the one you've given them license to enjoy.

Whenever you have a demonic spirit, it will be at your expense. They are not your friends!

We sometimes hear of familiar spirits. They show up as "friendly" and can look like your grandparent or a lost child. Sometimes they appear in your dreams. They are inviting, but let's end that now! If you are conversing with a familiar spirit, you are not talking with (or seeing) your friend or family member. You are engaging in an ongoing dialogue with a demonic spirit that is masking itself with your loved one's face and voice. It is very insidious, deeply cruel, and extremely malevolent. If you deal with that, don't be afraid. And don't give up, because you are about to get free. If that is you, pray this additional prayer:

Lord Jesus, I repent of anything dark and any sin that I have allowed in my life. I repent of anything binding me through my family bloodline and anything that has kept me in bondage—with or without my knowledge.

(Take some time to repent of any specific sin or habit that comes to mind as you are praying. Take an inventory of any issues with lust or greed involved with money, position, or any perversity. Confess it all to Jesus, and do not hold back.) Then continue with this:

Lord Jesus, I now hand the keys of my life over to You fully! I hold nothing back and trust You with my life. You gave Your life for me, even though You were innocent. I no longer give anything demonic any spiritual license to op- erate in my life. Instead, I apply the blood of Jesus Christ to my life—the blood that You, Jesus, shed on Calvary for me! I apply it to the doorposts of my life and accept You as both my Savior and my Lord. May You justify and shep- herd me in my new life with You. May no other lead me but You through the Holy Spirit of Christ in me. I am now a new creation in You. Amen!

Alright then! The groundwork is now laid for this discussion. The Holy Spirit has incredible truths to reveal to us, so be forewarned. When that happens, distractions of every kind will chase after us in an effort to interfere. Resist him and all his enticements. You are a human being made in God's own image, with His breath within you. He loves you dearly! His revelations through His Holy Spirit and His Word are our never-ending treasure trove, full of delight and health. Our whole being earnestly cries out for more of Him! Nothing and no one can compare with Him! In Him, and Him alone, do we find truth.

The puppet master is a master of lies. In fact, all witchcraft is false. It truly is! We see this in the Bible clearly as God confronts the gods of Egypt and their magicians through Moses in Exodus 7. No matter what you've been told elsewhere, that's the truth—and we've all heard stories that gave us chills. However, even our grandpa's "true" camp stories from years gone by are fiction. Although the devil possesses a power, it's not even remotely like the power that comes from God. God's power can flow through us, bringing life to all it touches.

Witchcraft is just a knock-off of God-given revelation.

So why reach for an off brand? Why look for another? Why choose the watered-down version over the real?

First of all, witchcraft is enticing. It claims to be *illuminating*. Doesn't that sound mystical and alluring? It does, but let's remove any mystery from this demonic façade. Witchcraft is just a knock-off of God-given revelation. If you purchase a brand name product, you want it to be authentic. That's why you got that one in the first place. The power behind witchcraft is not God's, and His power is not for sale!

We do not enjoy being hoodwinked or lied to by another person, so why would we invite such a false power into our life and give it control and space? Witchcraft only parades itself as the real deal; it does not intrinsically possess real revelation. It only appears to do so. God alone can give us true revelation, but many will share things like this:

- That fortune teller or tarot card reader told me something only I knew!

- That medium had the same tics and voice quality as my dad!

- That Ouija board message or horoscope came true!

- That palm reader didn't even know me and told me answers to my questions before I even asked!

- That horror movie described something I experienced in my childhood. I mean it was just like that!

Did you get the chills by just reading those? That's how it works. After being dazzled by the show, let's look behind the curtain.

The things described in the statements above are considered the "lighter" things of witchcraft. Of course, they're just as dark as the rest; they just appear harmless. They are purely bait, set out with the malicious intent to wow (and chill) you deeper still. These are the gateway devices, traps, and schemes leading to the labyrinthine paths of his dark realm. Do not be fooled!

Deeper, darker witchcraft is there for the taking to those who choose it—leading all the way to the yawning mouth of the eternal hellfire where demonic spirits will eventually go (Revelation 19:20). If your church has not taught you about this, it is time to look at it because the Bible does teach about it. God's Word is Holy Spirit breathed. It is given for rebuke and correction and more (2 Timothy 3:16).

Remember that satan does not want us to walk in the fullness of the truth of God's Word. Through religious spirits and the spirit of offense, he will exert pressure on us to keep us away from God's true illumination—and especially God's freedom. If discussing this is offensive to you or makes you angry or uncomfortable, take a moment right now to pray again over the release from demonic influence.

When we get close to outing its position, it tries to hide within us to possess our thoughts and grip our heart with fear. Evict satan's minions once and for all, and get your God-given life back!

> Therefore if the Son makes you free, you shall be free indeed. (John 8:36)

Again, Jesus, we invite You into everything we say and do. You, and You alone, will be given glory for setting people free from these terrible chains of bondage.

God is gracious and gives us simple pictures to better comprehend the things that have bound us, our families, our communities, and our nation. Sometimes, as we are set free by the Lord, He gives us the necessary individual pictures we need so we can intercede for greater issues and problems for our family and friends and outward. The Holy Spirit grows us and leads us in this direction with a ripple effect that floods through our churches, communities, countries, and to the whole world! And if God is there, so is the puppet master, frantically trying to lasso another soul.

Power is the ever-elusive carrot dangled from the puppet master's string.

Wherever you find people, witchcraft is at work. It has multiple names and operates in every pillar of society imaginable, but it has one function—to lure people away from God. The devil does not want anyone to know God and His Christ. He hates God's Word, and in the same vein, willfully works to destroy our relationships with other believers too. He will do anything to keep people away from their salvation so they are destroyed with him instead of saved by God. He is truly malignant.

That paragraph covers it in a nutshell as they say. So what's in a name?

Witchcraft is the "craft" of witches. Oftentimes, particularly lately, now that their practices are more acceptable and mainstream, they refer to themselves as those initiated in "the craft." Sounds mystical, eh? Just claiming this distinction brings a witch to attention. Being a so-called member of the craft gives them a sense of prestige and control. For power is the ever-elusive carrot dangled from the puppet master's string. He is intent on luring them deeper, and deeper still, into a chasm of degradation!

Those who seek control through the witchcraft spirit are completely controlled by it themselves.

Basically anyone—the dabbling or the astute—has an earnest hunger for power. It may begin in one area of life, but it will seep into every area of life with a need to possess the whole person! Witchcraft will demand the total worship of another god, and it will not be Jesus! Witchcraft is a demonic spirit, old and wily. Without Christ, we cannot combat it.

Those involved in witchcraft are rebellious to the things of God. Their master is the devil, and they have developed an addiction to power. They are power junkies like their evil overlord! That sounds like a science fiction plot and even a little cheesy, but it's not.

It's interesting to note that those who seek control through the witchcraft spirit are completely controlled by it themselves. They are not free in their quest for power. There is real freedom—and real power too—only in Jesus. We can do everything with the power of God's Holy Spirit.

Here is a simple picture God gave me about witchcraft: When we want to make something, we go to a craft store and buy the supplies we will need to make whatever it is we want to construct. Spiritually, witchcraft is an attempt to purchase revelation. A person wants power, but doesn't want to follow God, so they go to a different purveyor for it. True revelation can only be given by God (Daniel 2:47). Additionally,

God's revelation cannot be purchased, and neither can the power of God be used for anything other than its holy intent, which is directed solely by the Holy Spirit. Witchcraft attempts to bypass God and get revelation another way. You can read about such a situation in 1 Samuel 28:3-20, which shows you the thinking and attitude of one involved in deep witchcraft.

Witchcraft shows up in many forms. It can show up in sexual relationships, but it often pops up looking harmless in friendly encounters when ideologies, spiritual pursuits, and mystical revelations are discussed. People can open themselves up to the demonic through positions in exercise, meditation, and even some breathing methods, specifically those that involve chanting or include demonic incantations woven into the lyrics of the music used. There is even a demonic form of the "laying on of hands" through which demonic spirits can enter if the person is a spiritual impostor in the church! Don't get me wrong, the laying on of hands is biblical and right, but it should be done with vetted spiritual leaders.

A person involving themselves in witchcraft is on a slippery slope to great spiritual darkness and confusion, but in Jesus Christ they are not without hope! With witchcraft comes many demonic helpers or spirit guides. All kinds of demonic influences can lead to possession inadvertently, so avoid horror movies, occult television shows, haunted houses, and gaming portals. Remember, the saboteur does not play fair. He is a deceiver.

There is nothing attractive about demonic spirits. They will pose as what you want them to be. If we could see demons in their true form, no one would want them. They are fallen beings, and no longer connected to their holy Creator. They are fully rebellious and evil—tortured torturers. And they know this! Anyone consulting with any kind of witchcraft is actually consulting a demon spirit. Don't ever call it something else. We must not allow any lying spirit to rename the demonic as harmless when it is actually deadly. We must not be gullible! The saboteur is a puppet master; don't let him pull your strings!

A demon is a fallen angel—part of the host that was swept from heaven in the rebellion so long ago. These demonic hordes operate in an "order" though they hate one another. They will jostle and fight with each other for superiority inside any human they seek to possess, especially when they can manipulate that human into giving up their spiritual rights through sinful activities of various natures.

When you engage in illicit practices not sanctioned by the Word of God, you give demon spirits the right to access your life, and you open yourself up to this potentiality. If you know you need help in this area, get it. Deal with it. Repent, and take care of it, for your own sake, and for Jesus's sake who loves you dearly! Jesus can deliver anyone from the power of the enemy.

Deliverance begins by confessing that place initially—even if it is something that was done to you *without your consent.*

You do this by naming the place of entry through which the enemy of your soul has found a foothold. Deliverance begins by confessing that place initially—even if it is something that was done to you *without your consent.*

The devil is foul. He doesn't play fair, so he will take whatever he can and enter your soul through it. He uses fear, rape, crime, sodomy, abuse, rage, unforgiveness, tragic accidents, genuine peril (including firefights and any wartime scenarios), as well as generational family habits to gain entrance. These also include adultery, fornication, masturbation, molestation, homosexuality, prostitution, abortion, alcoholism, perversion, substance abuse, anxiety, suicide, mental and physical infirmity, satanic ritual abuse, sorcery, witchcraft, murder, idol worship, and any history with a medium, palm or psychic reader, or tarot card use. And there are so many more!

All sin gives him an opening. The Holy Spirit will shine His light on any area in which we need help. We can trust that He knows the way to set us free. We need His skill in dealing with the one who stalks our soul.

The saboteur is a predator. In the created world, predators kill because they are hungry and in need of food to survive. They eat what they need and leave the rest for other animals, but they do not kill for pleasure. That is not the case with demonic forces. They are on a limited-time killing spree. You are merely a means to an end for them. They offer no intimacy, no warmth, no care—although they can mimic all of that. They offer no quarter, which means they show no mercy.

Even the dark power they do have is only lent to their victims in degrees, and that power comes at a horrific price. Each degree deeper bites off more of your humanity in order to gain more control and flood your soul with greater darkness. Additional demonic compatriots merely looking for temporary housing often show up too.

This is absolutely true. If you find this funny, that may be a sign you need to deal with God about it. This is a serious subject. Remember, the fear of the Lord is the beginning of wisdom. We want to treat God and His kingdom as the pearl of great price—not a trinket.

There are rank-and-file demons, and there are stronger ones that have greater force. None of them are a match for Jesus and His authority, but wisdom and caution and the necessary Holy Spirit guidance should be used to proceed in all encounters with demon spirits. On our own, we cannot handle them.

Darker witchcraft sometimes involves blood rituals. This is abhorrent to a holy God, which is precisely why the saboteur will draw you into it. If you have been involved in blood sacrifices of any kind, renounce them and openly repent before God for all of it. Bind the spirits—one by one—by name, and ask the Holy Spirit to cover you while you cooperate with Him to break every agreement you ever made with darkness. If this is you, you need to be with someone who is a trusted deliverance minister to help you. You need a Holy Spirit-led, Jesus-loving, Word-passionate Christ follower to stand with you through this process.

The more deeply involved you are in these practices, the more radical ending them will be for you. Friendships and associations based in the dark arts have to be completely broken—even if they have spanned many years. Those involved may not understand and can even turn on you. Ungodly sexual relationships must be cut off and *all* paraphernalia burned. There should be none in your house, car, workplace, or even worn as jewelry—all must go (especially generational heirlooms). Do not give them away or ask anyone to keep them if they are associated with witchcraft!

If you have buried things in your backyard, like potions, tokens, talismans, or art, get rid of them. Destroy any written incantations, idols, and anything occult. Don't concern yourself with how long it has been in your family, how much it is worth, or how a family member might be hurt by your actions. Just burn it. It is a weight that represents chains of spiritual slavery. Sweep your spiritual—and your actual—house clean! Keep nothing, not even clothing you've worn that reminds you of activities you did. Get rid of it all!

> **Once you have been delivered, relinquish all the trappings and wares of the craft, and don't keep even one item as a memento of that time in your life.**

To do this thoroughly, ask the Holy Spirit to bring things of this kind to your mind, and be obedient to Him when He shows you something. Do not brush away anything He says because you think you misheard Him. Better to err on the side of being clean before God than to leave any foothold for satan to re-enter your life in any way. Be vigilant about this.

Once you have been delivered, relinquish all the trappings and wares of the craft, and don't keep even one item as a memento of that time in your life. Surrender everything to Christ, and stand under the protective flow of Jesus's cleansing blood—offered without any reservation for you! Come to Him as you are, following the steps outlined here to help you not get tripped up by the evil one on your journey to Christ Jesus. Remember, the demonic traps, tools, and devices are meant to lure you back in. If satan sees you leaving his camp, he will pull out all the stops to keep you in his corner, but unlike God, he doesn't love you. Only Jesus loves you.

So if you are into witchcraft in one—or many—of its forms, and you want out, God's arms are open wide, just as the Father was to the prodigal son in Luke 15. If you are serious about finding an exit from witchcraft, you will find solace, healing, real peace, true power, and authentic truth that is free from deception in one place—in Jesus!

When you become a new creation in Christ Jesus, your vision has cleared because your heart has changed, and your thought life is cleansed. This is a lifelong and ongoing process, but it is worth every minute! The whole world will seem new. You evicted what was evil and invited the holy presence of God to come and live inside of you. He is the way, and the truth, and the life! You've discarded all that is old in exchange for the new. Amazingly, Jesus loved us even when we were sinners and paid the price for us. Praise God! Because of His actions, we can enjoy knowing God.

> The reverential fear of God mixed with love and fascination and astonishment and admiration and devotion is the most enjoyable state and the most purifying emotion the human soul can know.[12]
> —A.W. Tozer, *Whatever Happened to Worship?*

---

12. A.W. Tozer, *Whatever Happened to Worship?* (Christian Publications, 1985), 30.

Chapter 21

Blame-shifting Connoisseur

Let's get this crystal clear: The saboteur *always* blames God or His servants for his own ugly work. You can count on it. He blames God in a calculated attempt to defame God's character as well as that of His servants. (This does not apply to those genuinely guilty of religious hypocrisy.) The enemy does this to everyone everywhere.

> Blessed is the one who perseveres under trial because, having stood the test, that person will receive the crown of life that the Lord has promised to those who love him. When tempted, no one should say, "God is tempting me." For God cannot be tempted by evil, nor does he tempt anyone; but each person is tempted when they are dragged away by their own evil desire and enticed. (James 1:12-14 NIV)

Many other names nearly equally fit the bill for the unpacking of this aspect of the saboteur's deadly games. Each captures some aspect of his ruinous personality. As blame shifter, our feelings mean nothing to him. His every scheme is deadly. He possesses a primal lust that seeks to blame God and His people for the disastrous ending that is planned for him. His goal is to undermine everything that is good and right and lovely and pure.

> Finally, brothers and sisters, whatever is true, whatever
> is noble, whatever is right, whatever is pure, whatever
> is lovely, whatever is admirable—if anything is
> excellent or praiseworthy—think about such things.
> (Philippians 4:8 NIV)

Take a good look at this list. These things are eternally in God's heart! Therefore, the devil targets them specifically. He plots, so you will be damaged, and then stealthily moved to mistrust God. His plan is to get you to blame God for the terrible things you have suffered, believing God has done them to you. All the while though, he is the evil behind all these efforts to break you down. Sometimes, he'll simply attack, but most often he tries to wiggle these ideas in through sinful choices you, or another who affects you, have made.

One can only imagine the evil grin that steals across his face as he does these things to us. It's much like the cartoon version of "The Grinch Who Stole Christmas!" It is knowing, and it is strategic. Its purpose is to steal your joy, while simultaneously pointing an accusatory finger in the direction of God. Today is the day to deal with this unwanted hitchhiker.

R.D. Bullock used the word "suspicioner" to describe the devil. He loves to flick the first domino to make the rest fall; he upsets the flow. Ever the thwarter, he loves to push people in the same way. He wants people to think that no one is trustworthy. As with all partial truths, he's mostly right. Except for God! God is *always*—not sometimes—*completely* trustworthy. Do not be consumed with mistrust. At its root lies doubt.

> Come, let us worship and bow down. Let us kneel
> before the LORD our maker, for he is our God. We are
> the people he watches over, the flock under his care.
> (Psalm 95:6-7 NLT)

God is the true Shepherd and the One to whom we belong. In the garden, God had a conversation with the man, the woman, and the serpent. Let's look at just a portion of what was said:

And He said, "Who told you that you were naked? Have you eaten from the tree of which I commanded you that you should not eat?" Then the man said, "The woman whom You gave to be with me, she gave me of the tree, and I ate." And the LORD God said to the woman, "What is this you have done?" The woman said, "The serpent deceived me, and I ate." So the LORD God said to the serpent, "Because you have done this, you are cursed more than all cattle, and more than every beast of the field; on your belly you shall go, and you shall eat dust all the days of your life." (Genesis 3:11-14)

It's easy to trace the blame shifting in this passage. Adam infers that it's really God's fault because he (Adam) only *listened to the woman God "gave" to be with him.* In like manner, the woman blames the serpent.

Satan just does not know where to stop, and that is his undoing every time!

Unlike the others, note that God never asks the serpent what he has done. God was already aware of his crafty nature. God knew what was in satan. He'd dealt with his horrifying rebellion in heaven, so God was aware of his disastrous fall and his intent. God understood that the devil's disposition was warped in such a way that he was bent on his plan repeatedly.

That old serpent saw that this had worked for him just the way he had hoped: He had ruined something beautiful and good—the masterpiece of God. He had sent the entire human race careening off course!

In the end, he manipulated Adam to blame Eve and Eve to blame the serpent, and opened every avenue to blame God.

One truth expels all the cobwebs and redeems this hopeless situation—the last Adam, Jesus! Satan just does not know where to stop, and that is his undoing every time!

Satan is not God and does not sit on God's holy mountain. He cannot create anything. He will not, in the end, get anyone's worship. He can only try to corrupt good, but in the end, according to Philippians 2:9-11, every knee will bow, and every tongue will confess that Jesus is Lord!

There aren't many gods. Only one. The other "gods" are demonic spirits that love the worship of God's creation and want to keep you there in that delusion. Paul repeats something Isaiah the prophet wrote in the Old Testament:

> For it is written: "As I live, says the LORD, every knee shall bow to Me, and every tongue shall confess to God." (Romans 14:11)

> Therefore God also has highly exalted Him and given Him the name which is above every name, that at the name of Jesus every knee should bow, of those in heaven, and of those on earth, and of those under the earth, and that every tongue should confess that Jesus Christ is Lord, to the glory of God the Father. (Philippians 2:9-11)

This means that even satan and his demons will be forced to confess Jesus as Lord. Everyone who has followed God and loved Him, as well as those who have not, will also be in that number. How marvelous it is to recognize, then, the undeniable truth of God's Word. Knowing his time is short, the vicious saboteur works to damage everyone who proclaims and values the living Word's life-giving and life-sustaining qualities.

In John 4, Jesus told the woman at the well that the water He gave was living. That woman cried, "Give me some of that!" She was thinking practically. With living water, she wouldn't have to go to the well every day anymore, but Jesus wanted her going to the well daily. He just had a different sort of well in mind! He wants us to visit *His* well daily, recognizing that without our spiritual water received through His Holy

Spirit, we will be continually parched and dissatisfied by the widespread corruption around us.

Therefore, we must stay spiritually hydrated so we can abide in strong relationship with God. This world is not our final home. We do not want to mirror the nation of Israel in their continual complaining against God and His leaders, and yet we see this pattern in history over and over again. Reading God's Word and praying are not just religious exercises. They build the relationship we depend on. Just as our physical bodies do poorly and die without hydration, so too do our spiritual ones!

> Most men will proclaim each his own goodness, but who
> can find a faithful man? (Proverbs 20:6)

We must not get snagged in the puppeteer's ropes and harnesses. He wants us in a position where we firmly believe that we are in the driver's seat and in full control. Think again!

In business, there is a tactic known as the "poison pill." In essence, when a company feels threatened by an unwelcome take-over bid, they try to make themselves seem less attractive to the bidder. The saboteur loves victims, but he doesn't love you. There's a difference. If he shows up wearing any of his many hats, it will never be for your good! He will also never show up as himself; he'll be wearing a disguise. He has many faces, but one aim.

He runs his demonic marketing team better than any other. Every generation has had its own "poison pills" served up to them, expertly packaged and appealing to their flesh in every way possible.

He is trying to outwit people, so don't give him your brain, your heart, your body, your soul, your strength, or your spirit! Do not be another one of his victims because you think you can handle him. He will handle you instead. On our own without God, we cannot outsmart him and his wily, old ways. We must have the Holy Spirit of God to light our path. Jesus told us to do the opposite of what the saboteur recommends:

"And you shall love the LORD your God with all your heart, with all your soul, with all your mind, and with all your strength." This is the first commandment. And the second, like it, is this: "You shall love your neighbor as yourself." There is no other commandment greater than these. (Mark 12:30-31)

Keeping the first of these commandments enables us to do the second. These commandments come from the Old Testament Law found in Deuteronomy 6, 11, and 13.

Those who invite the Holy Spirit to lead them will be enabled to expose the blame shifter for what he is.

Let's get back to the poison pill analogy. As the saboteur operates in this manner, every generation has a group *peeled away* from its root system in Christ's timeless truths. Whatever he's offering is an offering of death. It might be packaged in a chocolate box, but read the small print. Don't ignore the facts and don't ignore history.

We must not be lazy with our spiritual well-being. It's important. Our spiritual state determines where we will spend eternity. Those who invite the Holy Spirit to lead them will be enabled to expose the blame shifter for what he is. He's not cool or stylish; he doesn't have anything new and wonderful. He's still singing the same old tired song; he's just tweaked it for the next generation to try to put them on his slippery slope to death. Thank God that He saves us from this when we believe in Jesus.

But what does it say? "The word is near you, in your mouth and in your heart" (that is, the word of faith which we preach): that if you confess with your mouth the Lord Jesus and believe in your heart that God has raised Him from the dead, you will be saved. For with the heart one believes unto righteousness, and with the mouth confession is made unto salvation. (Romans 10:8-10)

Again, the terms used to highlight the saboteur's tactics were chosen to shine a light into his darkness. God wants us to make wise decisions over these areas that the devil deliberately seeks to keep hidden. Blame shifting is one of the initial roles we see satan in as he peddles blame—selling the idea to you whenever he can.

What will it be today? If we know this is how he functions, we can be ready for it, and able to reject every one of his plans, thereby making them ineffective.[13]

It is important to stay in the presence of God. By choosing purposefully to stay in God's presence, you stay slick with the oil of His holiness, and the places that the enemy used to get a grip on in your life will not be vulnerable like before. What a marvelous mental picture of an actual spiritual principle!

> Help, LORD, for no one is faithful anymore; those who are loyal have vanished from the human race. Everyone lies to their neighbor; they flatter with their lips but harbor deception in their hearts. (Psalm 12:1-2 NIV)

> Wisdom will save you from the ways of wicked men, from men whose words are perverse, who have left the straight paths to walk in dark ways, who delight in doing wrong and rejoice in the perverseness of evil, whose paths are crooked and who are devious in their ways. (Proverbs 2:12-15 NIV)

When you feel like sin is attempting to bring you down, ask God's Holy Spirit to redirect your faulty thinking, since you know those thoughts are not from God. Remind yourself to get covered in righteousness and

---

13. See 2 Corinthians 10:5-6

right thoughts in God's presence. Find psalms that speak to whatever you are dealing with, and pray them aloud, asking for God's peace and presence to prevail.

Chapter 22

Destroyer of Destroyers

They had as king over them the angel of the Abyss, whose name in Hebrew is Abaddon and in Greek is Apollyon (that is, Destroyer). (Revelation 9:11 NIV)

The saboteur is an assassin with a catalogue of methods he uses to achieve his ends. He does not possess creativity though. What some dub creativity on his part is simply the result of centuries of effort he has put into his evil craft. That is not creativity, it's cunning. Creativity begets life. The saboteur is all about death. Remember that. When you become familiar with his diabolical wares, you can thwart a good deal of the schemes and devices that have been set against you or others you love.

The hired hand is not the shepherd and does not own the sheep. So when he sees the wolf coming, he abandons the sheep and runs away. Then the wolf attacks the flock and scatters it. (John 10:12 NIV)

Satan is looking to stir things up; he wants to wreck things.

One day the angels came to present themselves before the LORD, and Satan also came with them. The LORD said to Satan, "Where have you come from?"

Satan answered the LORD, "From roaming throughout the earth, going back and forth on it."

Then the LORD said to Satan, "Have you considered my servant Job? There is no one on earth like him; he is blameless and upright, a man who fears God and shuns evil."

"Does Job fear God for nothing?" Satan replied. "Have you not put a hedge around him and his household and everything he has? You have blessed the work of his hands, so that his flocks and herds are spread throughout the land. But now stretch out your hand and strike everything he has, and he will surely curse you to your face." (Job 1:6-11 NIV)

The saboteur is an assassin with a catalogue of methods he uses to achieve his ends.

If you think this would turn out differently for you today, you are wrong. It wouldn't. If satan thinks God delights in you, you will quickly become his favorite target. Perhaps you feel like you already are, and you are trying to change that by reading this book.

The LORD said to Satan, "Very well, then, everything he has is in your power, but on the man himself do not lay a finger."

Then Satan went out from the presence of the LORD. (Job 1:12 NIV)

I have read this passage many times over the years, and I've always thought satan must have felt as if he had just been given the car keys so he could wreck it. You can almost feel the broil of rebellion and delight he gets from his presumed license in this situation. Clearly the devil no longer resembles what he was originally created to be. He is now completely foreign in nature to the pure, holy essence of God's character, which is full of light. The saboteur's nature, his outlook, and his unremitting goal is now broken, twisted, and hateful. Here you find an angry and aggressive spoiler eager for a fight.

Sometimes I think we read these Bible passages as though they are fables. We write them off as though the very real human tragedies and triumphs they describe didn't really happen, but that's not true. They aren't just good stories! Let's take away the teaching points and think about the complete malevolence behind what was happening to Job. How horrifying! We simply don't want to believe there is a real being who would think and do such things. Instead, we prefer to view him lightly as a fictional character. Because of this, the biblical narrative is of less value to us. We must never relegate God's Word to a tale or ancient lore.

The truth is that Job was a righteous man who was sifted by satan in every way possible, short of taking his life. It's time to get into the nitty-gritty of God's Word! Job was a real man whose family members died tragically. Then, satan attacked him further. Take the time to read this epic volume told from the Holy Spirit's perspective through Job. The book of Job contains copious details about corrupted man, sin, arrogance, self-righteousness, God, identity, and His power and might, along with the insidious nature of a conniving foe set on destruction. Job also had some rather interesting friends who did not serve him well. Still, Job fought hard and sought hard through it all to honor God.

Even so, the destroyer of destroyers attacked him in many ways. One was through words.

> The tongue also is a fire, a world of evil among the parts of the body. It corrupts the whole body, sets the whole course of one's life on fire, and is itself set on fire by hell. (James 3:6 NIV)

The things that come out of our mouth can do real damage, and that includes gossip, malice, slander, backbiting, lying, false testimony, boasting, blasphemy, and sinful jesting. This kind of devastation is one of the saboteur's specialties. That's why James warns us about it. The saboteur uses our words to throw a match on the gasoline-slick surface of those sins we habitually refuse to take to Jesus. The enemy is a destroyer of destroyers. Words hurt people. Unlike the children's song, words can be used like sticks and stones to incur real pain.

The saboteur uses our words to throw a match on the gasoline-slick surface of those sins we habitually refuse to take to Jesus.

They are a weapon of the evil one, who loathes our every breathing moment. Each of us should take stock of how we use our tongue. Read James 3 when you have a moment. We don't want to be pawns in the devil's hands. Instead, let's be Jesus's mouthpiece and a fountain of life!

Acts 8 gives some insight into another of the destroyer's attributes:

> Philip went down to a city in Samaria and proclaimed the Messiah there. When the crowds heard Philip and saw the signs he performed, they all paid close attention to what he said. For with shrieks, impure spirits came out of many, and many who were paralyzed or lame were healed. So there was great joy in that city. (Acts 8:5-8 NIV)

Philip performed many miracles. So did Peter and Paul, and that is a long, long list. After Jesus ascended into heaven and the Holy Spirit came, the miracles of God continued to flow, and they did not stop with that generation. In fact, they have never stopped, but they have been attacked. Unfortunately, that attack has had the ability to suppress them.

How could such a thing happen? Those who don't believe miracles still happen today have been *taught* to believe that way. This unbelief is a subject we've looked at before. Other *religious* men and women taught them to *not* believe. Jesus spoke about unbelief a lot. The religious leaders of His time were steeped in it. So Jesus dealt with it constantly. Do a word study on it sometime to see how Jesus dealt with it and what He thought about it.

The point is that this parched doctrine should be removed from the church. Instead, we can hold fast to our belief in Jesus and all He gives us: repentance, salvation through the cross, and a restored relationship with the living and powerful God. We can enjoy the assurance of sonship and the certain promise of eternal life, in addition to the outward signs of His inward work through the gifts and fruit of the Holy Spirit—and through *miracles*.

And what's so important about miracles anyway? Let's read what Jesus said about the miracles He was doing:

> If I do not do the works of My Father, do not believe Me;
> but if I do, though you do not believe Me, believe the
> works, that you may know and believe that the Father is
> in Me, and I in Him. (John 10:37-38)

Miracles have a purpose. God's miracles drew masses of people to Him. How joyous it must have been to see so many people set free and made whole. Later, Paul wrote that miracles were part of his ministry.

> I persevered in demonstrating among you the marks of
> a true apostle, including signs, wonders and miracles.
> (2 Corinthians 12:12 NIV)

Miracles attest to the power and love of God for mankind as He chooses to bring help that no one else can. In his assault on God's people, the enemy has worked stealthily through religious spirits to teach lies and sow doubt. In his mind, miracles—the powerful signs to the power of God that they are—have to be stopped! As the destroyer, he is focused on our words and what we believe most of all.

Let's take a moment to marvel at the plan and power of God instead. Jesus died and rose again for us. He wants us to know Him as the risen and powerful Lord and Savior that He is. Ask Him to show you any way that you need to submit to Him, either in your words or your beliefs. You've got this! May you be encouraged to walk as a believer in every way.

Back to the miracles: It was also doubt and unbelief that prevented miracles from happening in Jesus's time (Mark 16:14). What we believe really affects our faith. If we decide that Jesus can't heal, we are believing the doctrine of men over God. The Bible says He does heal. If we believe He does not do miracles, the Bible disagrees.

For the past several decades, the church has witnessed an open assault—even at the seminary level—in this area. Such faithless teaching is not in line with the Word of God. It is the work of satan through those wishing to elevate themselves and their supposed knowledge over the deeper understanding of what the Holy Spirit, who animates the living Word, says.

What kind of gospel have we received if it merely recounts the miraculous but has no power?

And there's more to it. The ridiculous notion that Jesus cannot heal today is a direct result of believing that Holy Spirit baptism is also not real and no longer occurs today as it did in the early church. It's heartbreaking to consider that many from that time and through the centuries gave their lives so the church (the body of Christ) would grow and thrive. They wanted it to be alive and full of vitality to this very hour.

No one wants to look Jesus—or any of the saints, prophets, or martyrs—in the eye and tell them that the sacrifice they made so we could pass along this golden thread of life did not matter. We need to look at what we believe. Who told you this? It was not Jesus or His Holy Spirit, or any of that large crowd of witnesses that has gone before us.

What kind of gospel have we received if it merely recounts the miraculous but has no power? Jesus never meant for us to wistfully read about the miraculous and not engage in it. He knew His power would be made manifest in every one of His followers as they had need. That's why He came in the first place. Jesus is the great I AM, the Resurrection and the Life, and that's the truth. Let's live like we believe that!

Some mock those who believe in the baptism of the Holy Spirit. They infer that these are not stable and must look for experiences and feelings. This is an unkind misunderstanding.

In Matthew, Jesus spoke about the demeaning labels that the religious leaders of His time tried to foist on John the Baptist and Himself. He concluded with these words:

> Wisdom is justified by her children [works].
> (Matthew 11:19b)

> Wisdom is justified and vindicated by her deeds [in the lives of those who respond to Me]. (Matthew 11:19b AMP)

> Wisdom is shown to be right by its results.
> (Matthew 11:19b NLT)

What kind of results was He talking about? Jesus loved to heal and deliver people from demons in His ministry. Jesus loves to heal and deliver people from demons today too. Let's reread the end of that passage from Acts 8:7-8 in the Amplified Version:

> For unclean spirits (demons), shouting loudly, were coming out of many who were possessed; and many who had been paralyzed and lame were healed. So there was great rejoicing in that city.

What a marvel it is to read about this! But remember, the Bible isn't a storybook filled with fairy tales. These stories are here to remind us that Jesus is the same yesterday, today, and forever (Hebrews 13:8). Let the Bible build up your faith that Jesus is Savior, Healer, and Deliverer by the power of His Holy Spirit today! Imagine the rejoicing—not just for those who had been healed, but those who witnessed each life no longer bound by the destroyer of destroyers. Let's be a living church, as they were, despite our culture's dismissal of that power! This is our directive from Jesus:

> Jesus came and told his disciples, "I have been given all authority in heaven and on earth. Therefore, go and make disciples of all the nations, baptizing them in the name of the Father and the Son and the Holy Spirit. Teach these new disciples to obey all the commands I have given you. And be sure of this: I am with you always, even to the end of the age." (Matthew 28:18-20 NLT)

This is the Great Commission from the mouth of our Lord. Through His authority, we are to make disciples, baptizing and teaching them. Later, in Acts 9, we learn of Saul's healing and Holy Spirit baptism through the prophet Ananias.

> And Ananias went his way and entered the house; and laying his hands on him he said, "Brother Saul, the Lord Jesus, who appeared to you on the road as you came, has sent me that you may receive your sight and be filled with the Holy Spirit." (Acts 9:17)

That is quite the commissioning for Saul (Paul), don't you think? In Acts 13, on Paul's first missionary journey, we read this:

> When the Gentiles heard this, they were very glad and thanked the Lord for his message; and all who were

> chosen for eternal life became believers. So the Lord's message spread throughout that region.
>
> Then the Jews stirred up the influential religious women and the leaders of the city, and they incited a mob against Paul and Barnabas and ran them out of town. So they shook the dust from their feet as a sign of rejection and went to the town of Iconium. And the believers were filled with joy and with the Holy Spirit. (Acts 13:48-52 NLT)

The enemy hated Paul and incited a mob! He still does this stuff. Here's an illustration. A precious young boy I know had just pitched a fantastic game. In fact, it was his excellent pitching skills that had won the game for his team as he had so many times before. He has a gift. Following the game, a player from the other team slugged this precious young boy's pitching hand.

We don't expect the unadulterated meanness of the enemy. We'll call it anything else, but we refuse to call it out for what it is. Last time I checked, envy was not a fruit of the Spirit. Neither is rage, nor covetousness, nor hateful destruction. The demonic seeks to work through the flesh. The saboteur will never play fair.

When the light of your gifting shows (and it is for Jesus's team that you do your finest work), you are going to be immediately targeted.

This is why putting on the full armor of God is not a suggestion, any more than following the Ten Commandments is. Knowing what spiritual weaponry to use—along with when and how to use it—is vital for every believer who wants to be effective. A person can possess a sword and have no idea how to wield it. This fits far too many in the body of Christ today.

Some of us have been told that our sword should "stay in its sheath" through sermons that do not highlight the Holy Spirit's power. We're told there's really no need to use the Word of God in our time. We've been told that all the work has been done, which is only partially true. Partial truths are the saboteur's most fine-tuned labors, sown into the "hive-mind" mentality of many who are not awake to his work. Do not be fooled!

Christ Jesus commissioned His disciples into real service. Jesus said it is finished because He'd done the pioneering groundwork; without it, we can do nothing. However, He fully expected and challenged His church to take ground, not relinquish it.

All of Psalm 37 is powerful, but let's read verses 11-15:

> But the meek shall inherit the earth, and shall delight themselves in the abundance of peace. The wicked plots against the just, and gnashes at him with his teeth. The Lord laughs at him, for He sees that his day is coming. The wicked have drawn the sword and have bent their bow, to cast down the poor and needy, to slay those who are of upright conduct. Their sword shall enter their own heart, and their bows shall be broken.

Do you see what the wicked want to do to the poor and needy—particularly the upright? The devil is at the heart of it all.

Jesus said that the devil was a murderer from the beginning (John 8:44). Jesus didn't mince words about the devil's character and intent. He chose those words accurately. The church needs to wake up and stop ignorantly partnering with the adversary to be part of the destruction of other people—believers and non-believers both. The devil delights in using people's words to hurt others and in keeping people trapped in unbelief. He does both simultaneously.

> Instead, you yourselves cheat and do wrong, and you do this to your brothers and sisters. Or do you not know that wrongdoers will not inherit the kingdom of God? Do not be deceived: Neither the sexually immoral nor idolaters nor adulterers nor men who have sex with men nor thieves nor the greedy nor drunkards nor

slanderers nor swindlers will inherit the kingdom of God. (1 Corinthians 6:8-10 NIV)

Do not be deceived: God cannot be mocked. A man reaps what he sows. (Galatians 6:7 NIV)

We will bear the fruit that we sow, so if we choose to believe false doctrine, we will bear its fruit. If we adhere to doctrine that is not in God's Word, no matter where it is from, then we are no longer following God's Word. Period. So all ideas must be tested against how they line up with the Word of God. Whatever the source, be it a college, seminary, well-known teacher, or a blog you follow, we must be careful over what we believe. We want to be like this guy:

A [discerning] king who sits on the throne of judgment sifts all evil [like chaff] with his eyes [and cannot be easily fooled]. (Proverbs 20:8 AMP)

The Word of God is our strong tower. It exposes the enemy's plans as well as his demise.

The Word of God is our strong tower. It exposes the enemy's plans as well as his demise. What a mighty gift the Bible is for those who have ears that will listen, eyes that will see, and hearts seeking the Holy Spirit's guidance. Psalm 49 describes the demise of the saboteur and all who go with him in his way, in just a few lines:

This is the fate of those who are foolishly confident, and of those after them who approve [and are influenced by] their words. Selah. Like sheep they are appointed for Sheol (the nether world, the place of the dead); death will be their shepherd; and the upright shall rule over them in the morning, and their form and beauty shall be for Sheol to consume, so that they have no dwelling [on earth]. (Psalm 49:13-14 AMP)

Therefore, it is vital that we are following Jesus and not "another" spirit that would pull us in the polar opposite direction from the path of life. There are not many paths to God; there is only one.

Thankfully, God does not withhold the essential things we need to know to keep us safe from the snare of the fowler. He helps us.

> For You will not leave my soul in Sheol, nor will You allow Your Holy One to see corruption. You will show me the path of life; in Your presence is fullness of joy; at Your right hand are pleasures forevermore. (Psalm 16:10-11)

God understands our hardships. The psalms show that. When we are struggling with enemy oppression or see darkness at work in our life, read this psalm. It is the heart's cry of one who understood your plight and lived there. Oppression often hits hardest when God is trying to bring correction to us. The psalmist identified his affliction as God's wrath upon him, which is different in nature. The problem could be physical or mental, due to a rebellious heart issue, or something spiritual. In any case, God wants to help us with it. All Scripture is useful for these moments.

Take the time to speak to God and tell Him you'd like to make it through your situation but need help. Make the choice to fear Him above all the other voices tugging and warring with your soul for dominance. Let Him lead you back to His good pasture! Sometimes we feel like this:

> Your wrath lies heavy upon me, and You have afflicted me with all Your waves. *Selah.* (Psalm 88:7)

There are few adults who can say they have never felt such an onslaught of the soul. Pray and use Scripture to get right footing in a Savior who loves you powerfully and seeks your healing and restoration, in full, not in part.

Cast all your anxiety on him because he cares for you.
(1 Peter 5:7 NIV)

Go to Him speedily. Never let another person, or a demon using a person, tell you that God does not care for you. He loves you! Remember, the devil only deals in death, but Jesus offers life.

To fear the LORD is to hate evil; I hate pride and arrogance, evil behavior and perverse speech. (Proverbs 8:13 NIV)

If you do what is right, will you not be accepted? But if you do not do what is right, sin is crouching at your door; it desires to have you, but you must rule over it. (Genesis 4:7 NIV)

The Father heart of God is evident in this verse when He is speaking to Cain. Before the murder of his brother, God saw what was in Cain's heart and warned him. He was telling Cain to reach out to Him. God saw the inner struggle of Cain's flesh, the temptations it produced, and the way they were overshadowing his ability to make right decisions. God sees that with us too. And He continues to reach out today, just as He did then.

Satan may not be suggesting you murder your brother, but he is suggesting something. He's constantly doing that. So let's be aware of his ways. He wants to use us to hurt each other and destroy our testimony at the same time, so don't let him. He steals your time through social media, entertainment, toxic friends that waste your time, and distraction after distraction after distraction. He will subtly try to shift your priorities, making causes you care about deeply more important in your life than God. Or he will get you absorbed in your love life, especially with individuals who do not love God. He does not care *how* he destroys your faith and testimony, just as long as it is indeed destroyed, along with you. So take a look at any way the destroyer of destroyers is active in your life through unbelief specifically.

Dear Jesus, where I have let other voices crowd out Your voice, I am sorry. You must be the One who guides me in all my ways and thoughts. You are my God. You have bought me at great cost to Yourself. Thank You so much. When I was on my way to hell and utter destruction, You came to be the Savior of my soul through Your death, burial, and resurrection. I renounce any and every way that I have misread Your love, discounted Your heart, or listened to other voices that did not tell me the truth about Your love and care for me. Forgive me for not nurturing my spirit, which You gave to me. I understand that through the Holy Spirit's work in me, I can rule over that which seeks to destroy me and my faith. I thank You for Your powerful Holy Spirit. Please guide me and keep me, my Redeemer and Good Shepherd. Amen!

Chapter 23

Cloying Consumer

"Never enough! There's never enough!" rages this angry soul. My glass is half empty! I should have more! I should have better! I deserve what they have! I should have been given what they have! "X" stole it from me! I was robbed of what I should have! I want what I should have been given! I want it all back with interest!

This describes the gospel of envy. The Bible says this:

> You should no longer walk as the rest of the Gentiles walk, in the futility of their mind, having their understanding darkened, being alienated from the life of God, because of the ignorance that is in them, because of the blindness of their heart; who, being past feeling, have given themselves over to lewdness, to work all uncleanness with greediness.

> But you have not so learned Christ, if indeed you have heard Him and have been taught by Him, as the truth is in Jesus: that you put off, concerning your former conduct, the old man which grows corrupt according to the deceitful lusts, and be renewed in the spirit of your mind, and that you put on the new man which was created according to God, in true righteousness and holiness. (Ephesians 4:17-24)

Envy produces a blindness that grows into an emptiness. In a conniving and manipulative way, it works a mental corruption that thrives in an unfiltered heart, multiplying swiftly to consume any healthy "spiritual" tissue there. In time, an uncleanness washes over all else.

Your *mind* and *heart* are the juiciest objectives ever. The battle rages between a futile-thinking mind versus a spiritually renewed mind in Christ Jesus.

The cloying consumer uses temptation. It can begin as simply as the desire for more—or for what another person has. It may even start as a true need, but it becomes an ever-growing focus in your life. Like a large piece of furniture moved into a small space obliterates the view of anything else around it, it dominates your thoughts. The devil is never gratified! He sows his malcontent everywhere he can.

Covetousness and contempt for what we have are part of the saboteur's original sin collection. He wants to hang them in the gallery of our heart. Ingratitude comes with them, like a pervasive weed, wandering wherever it wants and intruding on the worship and praise due to God.

It's as old as the sin in the garden. He convinces us that "something is missing." Sound familiar? We need something God is not going to give us, so we must get it for ourselves. We want something that is not ours, so we lust after it. In this hothouse of growing greed, hatred and jealousy grow happily as partners, a planting of the evil one.

> Keep your heart with all diligence, for out of it spring the issues of life. (Proverbs 4:23)

> Would not God search this out? For He knows the secrets of the heart. (Psalm 44:21)

> No, in heart you work wickedness; you weigh out the violence of your hands in the earth. (Psalm 58:2)

Dissatisfaction over what you have been given only highlights the parts that you "lack." In their focus on getting those "missing pieces" all the time, people can no longer see the good around them. Neither do they note the daily gifts they receive or the light of God's love for them, even when it's operating at full throttle.

> My people come to you, as they usually do, and sit before you to hear your words, but they do not put them into practice. Their mouths speak of love, but their hearts are greedy for unjust gain. Indeed, to them you are nothing more than one who sings love songs with a beautiful voice and plays an instrument well, for they hear your words but do not put them into practice. (Ezekiel 33:31 NIV)

The devil is full of all kinds of greed. By nature, he is covetous. Covetousness is so loathsome to God that He put it in the Ten Commandments. Whoever declares that God's character reigns in them cannot live in greed, envy, or covetousness (Luke 12:15).

Anyone like this is not walking in accordance with God's Spirit. Greed is not just a vice and not just a bad habit—it is a death trap. Walking hand in hand with it is the same as cooperating with the enemy of your soul and will lead, as all sin does, to destruction (Mark 7:21-23; Isaiah 57:17).

> Having lost all sensitivity, they have given themselves over to sensuality so as to indulge in every kind of impurity, and they are full of greed. (Ephesians 4:19 NIV)

By now, you understand that the saboteur is perpetually dissatisfied, and those who adhere to his practices will always be the same. They will neverendingly cling to the belief that they have been robbed. They don't have enough. They never will. Their list is as endless as the satanic tidal wave that drives it!

Such thoughts lock God out. A person run by greed considers God incompetent. In a clever ploy orchestrated by satan, God is blamed for what the flesh covets and cannot have. Greed does not like any kind of waiting. It is impatient and demanding.

In such an atmosphere, eventually God is thrust aside, as the cloying consumer slips gleefully into position. He really wants control. All he wants is you, and he'll promise you anything to get you.

The saboteur gets to sit where God should be. He rises while God is pushed aside—now a lesser figure, perhaps even a "religious" one, behind selfish thoughts that eventually shut Him out altogether. God is only in the way. Instead, all energy chases after all our wants and needs and our ongoing, self-motivated pursuits.

> **In a clever ploy orchestrated by satan, God is blamed for what the flesh covets and cannot have.**

However, God's plans for us are good, and He told us how to walk in them by keeping in step with His Holy Spirit. The fact is that whether you are rich or poor does not matter. The saboteur will try to woo you, pointing out possessions, positions, and pursuits that are just beyond your reach in his spinning merry-go-round of futile offerings.

Have you ever witnessed an animal cock its head backward and swallow its food whole, sometimes without even chewing? You want to say, "Whoa! Slow down, buddy. You're going to choke on that!" This is a good illustration of greed.

There are many small steps that the devil uses to lasso your life in this direction. Greed, envy, and covetousness is a brokenness that must be dealt with honestly and with intentionality. God understands this and has made provision for it in His Word.

Through earnest prayer and intentional focus, this demonic weight can be removed from your life as you seek Him. God is a God of rescue, redemption, and healing. He loves you and will help you.

Have you ever seen a picture of yourself, and you did not like it because you didn't know you looked like that? Somehow, this picture revealed something that was unbecoming in one way or another, and showed a truth you were unaware of, or perhaps you just thought you covered it well.

Again, the liar comes continually to make his declarations over you. Many times, these inner conversations are about what you do not have, or what you should have, or what you used to have but now don't. He'll suggest manipulative ways you can get it, and before long, the picture is painted.

The more you give way to such thoughts, the clearer the image becomes. The devil tries to inject this picture in your mind through deceptive suggestions so you will eventually act on it.

> We demolish arguments and every pretension that sets itself up against the knowledge of God, and we take captive every thought to make it obedient to Christ. (2 Corinthians 10:5 NIV)

As believers in Jesus, you and I can call on Him. When we do, His Holy Spirit will assist us in *countermanding* the arguments, pretensions, and thoughts that belie the truth of God. He does this for us and those around us.

We act according to God's will for us, not the enemy's plans.

We act according to God's will for us, not the enemy's plans. The devil never shows us the fine print in his contracts. We do not think and act according to the images we allowed the cloying consumer to paint in our mind. We turn away from him and get back in touch with Jesus. Through Christ, we *take captive* every lie and throw it down. We ask the Holy Spirit to "take out the trash" for us, removing all greed, envy, and covetousness so we are not tempted to pick up where we left off.

When the apostle Paul wrote the words "take captive," he meant actively keeping the door of our mind shut to the devil's lies. This takes active participation; it takes praise, worship, thankfulness, feeding on the Word, fellowship with other believers, and giving ourselves to others, not just our own selfish pursuits. All of these things and more will assist in regaining any ground lost to the evil one.

Thank You, Lord, for the many ways You have redeemed my life from the pit of my own thoughts and the empty ways of the world. You, Lord, are my hope, and I thank You for keeping me anchored in You! In You I have a precious pearl of the greatest price. Thank You, Jesus, that I belong to a kingdom of great value—not one that is perishing as the things of this world most certainly are. Thank You that Your plans for me have always been good. I'm excited to be growing more and more in You. I thank You for my salvation, purchased for me on the cross, and for the power of the resurrection that resides in me as I call on Your name for help! Thank You that You hear my voice and answer as I earnestly seek You. Thank You for valuing me. Cause me to know You more and understand even better how great a salvation I have in You. Thank You, Jesus. You are my treasure! Amen.

If you think you have a problem with greed, envy, or covetousness, pray this prayer:

Lord Jesus, please root out any place these foul habits exist in my life or family line. I want Your nature growing healthy and sure inside of me! Help me right now. As Your child, I want to look like You and by the transformative power stated in Your Word I know that I can do this with Your help. I want You to operate in all of me, holding nothing back. I trust You as my Savior and Lord! Wash me of the sins of greed, covetousness, and envy. Go deep, Lord

Jesus! I promise to return to You every time I feel sin's voice attempting to speak to me. I will invite Your Holy Spirit to silence every contrary voice of corruption that I have allowed in my life. By Your Holy Spirit, cause these voices to become utterly foreign to me. May my new thinking in You take over, Jesus! Forgive and cleanse me of all unrighteousness in this specific area right now. Amen.

(If the Holy Spirit brings specific things to your mind, renounce the enemy's leverage over you in them. Leave no ground for him to return.)

Chapter 24

Paranoid Pawn

So will I choose their delusions, and bring their fears on them; because, when I called, no one answered. When I spoke they did not hear; but they did evil before My eyes, and chose that in which I do not delight. (Isaiah 66:4)

And with all unrighteous deception among those who perish, because they did not receive the love of the truth, that they might be saved. And for this reason God will send them strong delusion, that they should believe the lie, that they all may be condemned who did not believe the truth but had pleasure in unrighteousness. (2 Thessalonians 2:10-12)

Your prophets have seen for you false and deceptive visions; they have not uncovered your iniquity, to bring back your captives, but have envisioned for you false prophecies and delusions. (Lamentations 2:14)

Satan is both far more and far less than the big bad wolf or some other evil character from a storybook. He projects "omniscience" by stealing strategies from men and women to control humanity. In turn, God uses this fallen angel's paranoia to His own end. Satan is not omniscient. God genuinely loves people and wants *the best* for them. God loves life, and He is the only genuine Creator in the room.

Utilizing cutting-edge technology, even "artificial intelligence" to sweep up all the details he can't see, satan tries to convince people that he still has his old angelic abilities—but he does not. He once walked among the fiery stones of God in God's pure and glorious presence, where no impure thought could ever abide. Satan, like the rest of the angels and heavenly host, was privy to what God chose to share of Himself. The books of Isaiah and Revelation both give us a picture of this.

> Above him were seraphim, each with six wings: With two wings they covered their faces, with two they covered their feet, and with two they were flying. And they were calling to one another: "Holy, holy, holy is the LORD Almighty; the whole earth is full of his glory." At the sound of their voices the doorposts and thresholds shook and the temple was filled with smoke. (Isaiah 6:2-4 NIV)

Day and night they never stop saying:

> Holy, holy, holy is the Lord God Almighty, who was, and is, and is to come. (Revelation 4:8)

At Christmas in 2022, Pastor Kent released a word titled "The Midnight Cry"—a word given "in defense of the gospel of Jesus Christ." It was profound! He stressed that there has never been an hour in which the gospel of Jesus Christ has been under greater attack than the hour that you and I are in. But this assault does not come from outside, but from *inside* the four walls of the organized church today. Professors in our seminaries, best-selling authors, renowned pastors with PhDs, hirelings who are greedy for wealth and wolves in sheep's clothing who are only ego driven. The church today may be more educated, more refined, set in multimillion-dollar sanctuaries and have famous people in the pews, but we have become powerless and weak, holding a form of God but having no authority and no power.

The church that God Almighty birthed on the day of Pentecost with the blood of the darling of heaven, Jesus our Savior, looked like Jesus, talked like Jesus, acted and had the authority of Jesus, and made demons tremble and bow at His name. The messages today may fill buildings, but they put hell at ease! When did the Bible stop being the commandment of the Lord and just become suggestions? When did other things become more important than the presence of God? No wonder the Lord said that in the last days the love of many will grow cold. Contrary to the watered-down gospel being preached today, labeling yourself a Christian doesn't give you automatic access to heaven. Somebody lowered the bar in the United States. When it comes to serving the Lord Jesus Christ, though you may rewrite the Bible, and declare that it doesn't really mean what it says, Jesus said, "On that day, I will not judge you, but this Book, My Word, will judge you."

> Enter by the narrow gate. For the gate is wide and the way is easy that leads to destruction, and those who enter by it are many. For the gate is narrow and the way is hard that leads to life, and those who find it are few. (Matthew 7:13-14 ESV)

God alone is the Clock Master. He will orchestrate the seasons.

> And He said to them, "It is not for you to know times or seasons which the Father has put in His own authority." (Acts 1:7)

> Now concerning the times and the seasons, brothers, you have no need to have anything written to you. For you yourselves are fully aware that the day of the Lord will come like a thief in the night. While people are saying, "There is peace and security," then sudden destruction will come

upon them as labor pains come upon a pregnant woman, and they will not escape. (1 Thessalonians 5:1-3 ESV)

God's intercessor, prophet, and advisor to kings, Daniel, declared this:

Praise be to the name of God for ever and ever; wisdom and power are his. He changes times and seasons; he deposes kings and raises up others. He gives wisdom to the wise and knowledge to the discerning. He reveals deep and hidden things; he knows what lies in darkness, and light dwells with him. (Daniel 2:19-22 NIV)

There is a time for everything, and a season for every activity under the heavens. (Ecclesiastes 3:1 NIV)

And God said, "Let there be lights in the expanse of the heavens to separate the day from the night. And let them be for signs and for seasons, and for days and years, and let them be lights in the expanse of the heavens to give light upon the earth." And it was so. (Genesis 1:14-15 ESV)

How does this paranoid pawn manipulate you or I to succumb to this aspect of diabolical paranoia pulsating in his dark heart, yet so unrelated to the vital presence of the Almighty One, our King Jesus?

An outstanding example can, unfortunately, be found in the political arena of our day. One party will accuse the other party of doing what it's been doing. This practice is mean, malicious, and confusing. It paints the opposing party black, as it were, with *its own* hidden stain or sins. But with the enemy of our souls, there is no laundry soap for that! There is no spot remover save the very blood of Jesus Christ when we walk and work in the evil one's ploys and plots!

How many times have you heard from the lips of close friends and family, as well as the average stranger you meet every day, the *accusation* that God was the author of their trial or pain—unmindfully pouring from the lips of one who has lost a baby, a spouse, a son or daughter, a friend or girlfriend. That painful loss is easily dropped on God's doorstep like the shuddering offering of a dead mouse by a beloved cat or dog.

Before the accusation from your heart passes through your lips, pause and ask yourself why you repeat this untruth to others. God calls Himself the Author of Life (Acts 3:15) not the author of death. But it's critical to understand that God breathed His breath into man, and it is that which sustains each one of us. When we pass from this life to the next, God recalls our spirit to Himself. However, to blame God for things He did not cause (like accidents, mishaps, medical interventions that did not prove helpful, etc.) is a misrepresentation of God's character.

When one looks into the many misfortunes lain in God's lap, it's surprising to learn that the individual never attempted to draw close to God. Their excuses for not doing so usually revolves around the errors of "religion" or "religious people," specifically named denominations, or the total error of the Bible. These excuses are often scattered like so many droplets in an effort to justify the complete lack of their relationship with God.

There has to be necessary intentionality to refuse the paranoid pawn access to your soul. His attempts from his dark world will be many throughout your lifetime—an unrelenting obsession to trip up his prey. A dear friend of mine in my younger years used to say frequently, "But God..." and we'd both smile knowingly. This would follow statements of utter faithlessness made by a doctor or a friend, a just learned situation, and even critical, urgent, or time-sensitive emergencies.

Never, ever let the paranoid pawn dictate your prayer life.

Never, ever let the paranoid pawn dictate your prayer life. God never ceases to answer prayer, no matter if you think He is not listening, or He didn't answer the way you wanted Him to ninety-nine times before. God is a sovereign being with an intellect and a heart far more expansive than we could ever conceptualize in our human frame, and that hundredth time just might be *the kairos moment*. Trust God! Trust Him again, if you've ceased doing so.

It is the chief effort of the paranoid pawn to pull you into his wicked vortex of lies, complaints, discouragement, and endless doubt, confusion, hatred, anger, blame, and unforgiveness. Make a choice to *end it now*!

Chapter 25

Vicious Villain vs. Victorious Vanquisher

> Be sober, be vigilant; because your adversary the devil walks about like a roaring lion, seeking whom he may devour. (1 Peter 5:8)

Language is interesting. What one person reads with understanding, another misses altogether. While this verse may seem abundantly clear to me, another might overthink its content, and some will dismiss it entirely. Those are the people who *under*think, reading the Word passively.

"Be sober" has connotations of remaining in a state of alertness and awakened to the spiritual happenings around you. It refers to an awareness that we are dealing with both a natural and a *supernatural* world. Some Christian teaching isn't even convinced of that, but the Word—Jesus—made this fact abundantly clear. *Sobriety* also speaks directly to *not* being in a state of drunkenness or so inebriated that your thinking is impaired. This does not just apply to alcohol usage, but to anything that would cloud or darken your capacity to make wise or prudent judgments, both practically and spiritually.

It does not suggest that you do this occasionally. Be sober. Be vigilant. Both are commands.

To be vigilant is to be actively awake and to be aware of your surroundings. My husband used to put it this way, and though it makes me laugh, it also helps me to remember it. He says, "Keep your head on a swivel!" This is wise and practical advice.

Our Supreme Guide, King Jesus, knows the saboteur well. He knows that the enemy is skilled in sabotage and subterfuge. In battle, or a football game, or even in a business setting, we understand the need for preparation. Why is it, then, that we take so little time to heed Jesus who knows our enemy and his capabilities? Take a minute and ask Jesus to show you any ways in which you have not listened to His advice for you. Speak to Him directly and relationally, as you speak to a friend, saying, "I am sorry, Lord, for the time I did not listen and—" (fill in your own story). It's important that we own our rebellions and not just wave them off or justify them. This leads to patterns of rebellion to His Lordship before we're even aware we're in them.

Do not treat the saboteur like a kitten; he is a lion.

Our adversary the devil walks about like a roaring lion. There are no "maybes" in that statement. When it continues past the commands of sobriety and vigilance, it moves straight on to "because." There is no space given. The writer knew he was sharing truth here! You must know it too. To combat the saboteur, you must begin to tell yourself the truth about his character. He is a nasty, vicious, vigilant villain. He will not stop bothering you because you are a nice person. He will not stop because you are sick. He will not stop because you are sad or trying to get sober. He will pour it on in wicked strength and will not stop until he has destroyed you.

You do not play with a lion like you would a kitten. That sounds silly on paper, but some people think they can play silly games with a hungry predator. That's not too smart. It never ends well in the wild, and it does not end well in the supernatural realm either. Heed the Holy Spirit's warning through God's perfect Word: Do not treat the saboteur like a kitten; he is a lion.

Many Christians feel it necessary to point out that Jesus is the Lion of Judah. He certainly is! And God can stop the mouths of lions (which He has done and will do)!

To understand the ways of the saboteur does not diminish the might of God. Even so, you must know your enemy so that when you encounter him, you are prepared for his fighting techniques and are no longer vulnerable to his wily ways, his appetites, and the devices he uses to trap you and others you know and love.

David wrote this in his messianic song, speaking of what Jesus would endure hundreds of years after he wrote it:

> They gape at Me with their mouths, like a raging and roaring lion. (Psalm 22:13)

The enemy does not play fair. His human agents do not play fair either. They are as vicious as their villainous father (meaning the devil). Most of these individuals have unchecked character issues or are sporting demonic activity due to direct contact with the occult or rebellion in any number of areas.

The vicious villain hates children supremely. Just like a hungry lion tries to pick off the young and vulnerable, the sick or the feeble, so does he. He doesn't have a second thought about it. He's hungry, and he is going to feed on what is easiest to catch. In nature films, I always want to avert my eyes. Over time, you come to learn there is a natural chain of predators that are bigger and stronger than others. The lion, like some other large predators, has no real enemy to speak of that can defeat him. This is why he is often dubbed "the king of the beasts" or "the alpha predator."

As the Victorious Vanquisher, King Jesus reigns supreme over the dark realm. Yes, He does! Psalm 91:13 is powerful:

> You shall tread upon the lion and the cobra, the young
> lion and the serpent you shall trample underfoot.

This verse is there to lay claim to its truth in prayer. It is scriptural that you will need to do this. The devil will not stop being a predator because you think what he is doing is mean. Your feelings do not matter to him, much as a feeding lion couldn't care less about the baby cape buffalo he's tearing to pieces. Even though the hungry lion may have had a fight on his hands to get that meal, he has no regrets. The devil will attack whether you complain or not. We are not to be ignorant of the fact that he will devour us if he can—if we are not sober and vigilant. So keep your head on a swivel. Be prayerful always, not just sometimes. Prayer is a life-preserving and vital habit.

That vicious villain is looking for anything available in his surroundings as he walks around—never satisfied and ever hungry.

Where, in your life, might you be giving that hungry lion leeway? Are you giving him any latitude or margin?

Evil will always be the particular work of the vicious villain.

> He lies in wait secretly, as a lion in his den; he lies in wait
> to catch the poor; he catches the poor when he draws him
> into his net. (Psalm 10:9)

This is not just talking about those with no money. A person can be poor in the things of the spirit too. These are the ignorant or unbelieving, and he lies in wait for them!

How did that hungry lion get a hold of your children? How did that hungry lion get a hold of you? How did that hungry lion ravage your family life and your family line? If you do not know, ask the Holy Spirit, but my guess is that you do know. Most people know. However, sometimes the deceitfulness of sin can darken your ability to read a situation correctly.

Ask the Holy Spirit to show those places of vulnerability to you right now. Do not move past this point until you get some clarity. Deal with it right now by calling on the Lord Jesus. Repent of any door(s) you left open for that hungry lion to enter. Leave no sacred cows on the table! Put them all on the altar before a Holy God who wants to help you and do good for you.

Ask the Holy Spirit to help you shut the spiritual door that allowed that ravening beast into your life! (The only name you need to call on is Jesus. If you have asked other gods to be lord over you, you must first repent of that. God will share space with no one!)

David cried out these words of prayer in song:

> My soul is among lions; I lie among the sons of men who are set on fire, whose teeth are spears and arrows, and their tongue a sharp sword. (Psalm 57:4)

Jesus will come to our aid as the Vanquisher. David wrote:

> Break their teeth in their mouth, O God! Break out the fangs of the young lions, O LORD! (Psalm 58:6)

> Save Me from the lion's mouth and from the horns of the wild oxen! You have answered Me. (Psalm 22:21)

Sometimes we don't know how to pray because the vicious attacks are swift and have hit the mark so many times we feel as if we have been felled already. We are badly wounded and can't see a way to get back up on our feet. This is why we have a Savior who can fight at that level for us. Jesus fights on our behalf, but not if we are complicit with the enemy. We must relinquish our fence-riding ways. We can't date the devil while calling on the Lord! As we recognize Jesus as the only way, He will come in His saving capacity.

Chapter 26

Subversive Stratagems

Do you truly want to break the master of subterfuge's chokehold on your life and stop being manipulated by his stratagems? Ask yourself that, and really think about it. If you are still filled with unbelief regarding God's supreme power and nature working in and through you, that load of unbelief is the real enemy in your life. It will be hard for you to move one inch until you reconcile that. If you feel insulted, examine your heart. Many people say they believe in God, but their life does not show it. Does yours?

Through his subterfuge and stratagems, satan steals, kills, and destroys. He has done that—and will continue to do that—for as long as we allow. If you remain ignorant or apathetic to his devices, you will make it easy for him. Let's take a look at one of satan's most successful stratagems.

One of satan's ploys is the use of slogans to engineer both mind and heart control. In marketing and sales, slogans can make or break a product's viability and success. And that's the bottom line. It's really very simple, and people in serious sales work will tell you the simpler ideas are often the better ones.

The saboteur will get believers to fight other believers. He will also move believers to stand behind non-believers on matters that are unbiblical. He manipulates God's people to put his arguments in our mouth! Christians fight against other Christians and stand alongside those who openly do not believe in God's truth as written in His Word.

Here's the real question: Why are God's people putting satan's filthy words into their mouth? Good question. How did those ideas get in there? Through our mind and heart (the soulish realm), that's how. We allow them in, and then they emerge as satanically manipulated thoughts that "win over" other "converts" to the cause.

This occurred right under our nose because we did not recognize the manipulator for who he is. We exchanged God's truth for a lie. When we recognize that we have done this, we must be faithful to God and take it to Him in repentance. Here's a prayer to get you started:

Lord, forgive me for letting that lie into my mind and heart. I repent right now for allowing the devil's subtle manipulation to permeate my thinking when the Holy Spirit has been given to me as a gatekeeper for such things. Forgive me for bypassing His voice and listening to my own thoughts instead, or for placing another voice over Yours. Forgive me for allowing myself to be convinced that I was being "intolerant" to think as Your Word directs. Always keep me vigilant in this area as I seek to become more like You. Amen.

The saboteur will do literally anything to get you off the track of Jesus in your life. Remember that!

We read in Luke 10 that Jesus sent out the seventy, two by two, and gave them a mandate to go into every city where He would go. They returned with joy, saying, "Lord, even the demons are subject to us in Your name." This was His response:

> I saw Satan fall like lightning from heaven. Behold, I give
> you the authority to trample on serpents and scorpions,
> and over all the power of the enemy, and nothing shall by
> any means hurt you. (Luke 10:18-19)

These words are as true for us today as when Jesus spoke them to the seventy. These disciples marveled that the demons were subject to the name of Jesus, but Jesus responded by telling them who He is. He was there when satan fell from heaven. When we know who Jesus truly is, we will know who we are, and there will be no room in our life for unbelief.

God has an answer for every subversive scheme and evil plan the saboteur devises and attempts to put into action, and the agency through which He thwarts those plans is the church.

When this revelation firmly takes hold of you and me, God will begin to do amazing things through us. It is happening now—the bride of Christ is emerging to defeat the stratagems of the enemy. God has an answer for every subversive scheme and evil plan the saboteur devises and attempts to put into action, and the agency through which He thwarts those plans is the church. We oppose him in every way possible. We do not need to be afraid of the devil; we only need to fear God, and it will go well for us.

> In the fear of the LORD there is strong confidence, and
> His children will have a place of refuge. (Proverbs 14:26)

In Acts 10, Peter is speaking to a non-Jew, a man referred to in the Bible as a gentile. In fact, Peter needed a holy encounter to even get him to go to Cornelius's house because Jews did not stay with gentiles. (Read the whole chapter!) However, because of that holy encounter and Peter's obedience to the Holy Spirit, something outrageous occurred. This is the kind of thing the saboteur does not want us to do. When we listen to the Holy Spirit and act on what He tells us, things happen. Why?

Because you are serving God—not serving yourself or the enemy—and God wants to partner with you in the same way.

> Then Peter began to speak: "I now realize how true it is that God does not show favoritism but accepts from every nation the one who fears him and does what is right. You know the message God sent to the people of Israel, announcing the good news of peace through Jesus Christ, who is Lord of all. You know what has happened throughout the province of Judea, beginning in Galilee after the baptism that John preached— how God anointed Jesus of Nazareth with the Holy Spirit and power, and how he [Jesus] went around doing good and healing all who were under the power of the devil, because God was with him." (Acts 10:34-38 NIV)

Peter did not withhold this information from this devout man—or any who were gathered in his house. Peter shared the gospel just as he understood it because he no longer lived for himself. Peter understood that he was God's servant.

We do not need to be afraid of the devil; we only need to fear God, and it will go well for us.

Since Jesus did good by healing all those under the power of the devil, Peter did too. Following Jesus's pattern, Peter taught, preached, and obediently did what Jesus had done in leading others in the truth. The Holy Spirit was leading him, as Jesus said He would.

Just before going to Cornelius's home, the Holy Spirit taught Peter what He needed him to know. So simple. We must do the same. Follow Jesus's pattern, not the pattern of this world. We left that behind when we chose to follow Him.

"Behold, I have created the blacksmith who blows the coals in the fire, who brings forth an instrument for his work; and I have created the spoiler to destroy. No weapon formed against you shall prosper, and every tongue which rises against you in judgment you shall condemn. This is the heritage of the servants of the Lord, and their righteous is from Me," says the Lord. (Isaiah 54:16-17)

This book came as the result of urgent, Holy Spirit prompting. That means the Holy Spirit wants us to listen and move as He tells us to move. He has been faithful to us, and we can trust Him to lead us.

May God himself, the God of peace, sanctify you through and through. May your whole spirit, soul and body be kept blameless at the coming of our Lord Jesus Christ. (1 Thessalonians 5:23 NIV)

About the Author

Heather Otis Tayloe is the daughter of an evangelist and Bible teacher, and she is the mother of three grown children and grandmother. She and her husband, John, have been married for thirty-eight years. She is a California native and graduate of CSUN with a B.A. in Journalism and an accompanying minor in Religious Studies. Co-founder of an international missionary radio network with John, she is the producer and host of three radio programs, running for several years which included "Discoveries in Prayer" and "Night Watch" along with her latest, "The Cowboy Church" on their local 99.1 FM The Ranch in Simi Valley, California.

Her radio experience includes multiple commercial voice-overs, and she has been involved as a Bible study and prayer ministry leader locally for over two decades. She has created prayer curricula for a parent prayer group for a major university and authored dozens of biblical character studies, including one for middle school-aged children. She also worked with high school girls as a small group leader. Heather is a poet and written word author, as well as an artist in both the acrylic and watercolor mediums.

Heather can be contacted at htayloe@saboteurbook.com or by visiting www.saboteurbook.com.